Core Competencies:
Real options as corporate strategy

Robert Hughes

A publication in the Creating Business Angles Series.

Core Competencies: Real options as corporate strategy
by Robert Hughes

Published in 2021 by Hughes Books an imprint of Hughes Consulting Limited
NZ Business number 9429038579288
UK Registered number 05067369

www.HughesBooks.info

Alpha Edition
© Robert David Hughes 2021

This book is copyright. Apart from fair dealing for the purpose of private study, research, criticism or review, permitted under the Copyright Act 1994, no part may be reproduced by any process without the prior permission of the copyright holders and the publisher.

ISBN 978-0-473-61100-2 (Paperback)
ISBN 978-0-473-61101-9 (Epub)

A catalogue record of this book is available from the National Library of New Zealand Te Puna Matauranga o Aotearoa.

Contents

Introduction   1

Chapter 1
The context for the emergence of core competencies   10

Chapter 2
Characteristics of production processes   26

Chapter 3
The imitability of core competencies   49

Chapter 4
Rarity of core competencies   58

Chapter 5
Managing a portfolio of salient real options as corporate strategy   74

Key influences on the work   77

Glossary   78

List of figures

Figure 1
Decision tree of features of core competencies — 6

Figure 2
Illustrative value network map for parcel delivery services showing market share and key players at different periods of time and the macro-trends driving change — 15

Figure 3
Illustrative heuristic market supply curve for a competitive market with four main/types of providers with implied relative average unit costs — 18

Figure 4
Example of financial information used to estimate planned unit gross margin and average unit cost — 20

Figure 5
Value-for-money indifference, demand and market supply curves for products with different perceived benefits — 23

Figure 6
Activity type matrix with description of products produced and associated sources of declining cost economies — 28

Figure 7
Questions to establish candidate delivery and acquisition methods — 31

Figure 8
Comparative operational features of five types of assemble delivery method operations processes — 33

Figure 9
Business implications of five assemble delivery method operations processes — 34

Figure 10
Capabilities and information flow diagram for a parcel delivery service using the aggregate-assign activity type — 37

Figure 11
Comparison of some operations process capabilities used in the production of statistical information against a hypothesised ideal process — 38

Figure 12
Decision tree to establish state of expertise — 41

Figure 13
Illustration of scope of interaction between four knowledge domains — 43

Figure 14
Influence diagram of a high-level ideal resilient production process (applied to the product market perspective) — 53

Figure 15
Assessment of the actual capabilities of a simple parcel delivery service — 55

Figure 16
Scope of the change in the constituents of the business angle by development strategy with examples of high-level development strategies available to a simple parcel delivery organisation — 62

Figure 17
Activity type matrix showing alternative business angles for a courier business — 72

Introduction

Application

An organisation's value is derived from its scarce resources and success in speculating. Where an organisation's production process is more profitable than competitors, then it has developed core competencies in the production process. Core competencies are not only a resource generating profit, they are also a scarce resource. An organisation with no core competencies has no value (other than the liquidation value of its assets) and remains in business for as long as it has the funding to do so, or if it suits competitors to keep it in the market. There are several reasons for being interested in the subject of core competencies, the main ones being to:

- Design ways to create new core competencies. For example, new ventures entering a market want to be able to create scarce resources. Demonstrating that a new venture has some prospect of creating value is critical to its success and ability to attract new funding.
- Leverage existing core competencies into new business angles. This may be crucial to extending the life expectancy of an organisation and gaining a return on existing core competencies. This option is used by organisations that have created scarce resources, where the best way to monetarise them is through the continuity of the organisation.
- Maintain and increase the value of existing core competencies. This is a preoccupation of organisations faced with capital budgeting constraints, and getting the right balance between the different demands for capital is important. A danger is to invest too little in maintaining and enhancing core competencies, and too much on high risk 'shiny' new initiatives, thereby reducing the value of the organisation. Knowing where to apply capital expenditure matters.

- Steer business transformation in response to changes in market conditions. These responses might extend to adopting outsourcing to acquire inputs or even the entire product, or a new labour model. Both these examples can change the activity type used by the business and should be accompanied by redesigned production processes. Failure to frame business process transformation as a change in activity type adds risk, by making the enhancement of core competencies a matter of chance.
- Guide turnaround managers of businesses under financial stress, enabling them to identify the organisation's core competencies to safeguard their value, and ensure they are not destroyed in the drive to re-establish profitability.

This book sets out an approach to identifying core competencies and evaluating their current and potential value. Building on this, it also looks at the different ways that core competencies can be improved or undermined by changes: in the value network; from management decisions; or imposed by social, economic and environmental trends. The book makes the case for the use of core competencies to create real options as the foundation for corporate strategy.

The business angle and production processes

Production processes (sometimes called the production function) deliver products to exploit perceived business opportunities, and they are a component of the business angle. A business angle encapsulates the perceived business opportunity and the way that it is to be realised through an activity type that is embodied in a production process. An activity type consists of capabilities and supporting information to deliver planned outputs from acquired required inputs. There are 16 sentinel activity types. In principle, each of these activity types can be used to design a quite different way to share in the expected value added associated with a perceived opportunity. An activity type is an element of a production process. Production processes have organisational structure, activity type that uses production technology with appropriate knowhow, systems and processes, information, resources, and contractual obligations to transform inputs into deliverable outputs. In a market different production processes, embodying different activity types, compete with one another for a share of the available value added from a perceived business opportunity.

Relationship between core competencies and business value

Various methods are used to value businesses. One method is based on ability to earn profits into the future. This is the Future Cash Flow (FCF) method of calculating the implied value of a business. The implied value is the net present value of expected income for the expected expenditure made, over its lifetime. Expected income and expenditure includes that from speculation and the ability to manage uncertainty. Present value is the value today of a future amount taking into consideration the time value of money. The time value of money is the discount rate. Adding the present values of all expected cash inflows and outflows for all periods over a venture's lifetime gives the net present value. In the simple example, a $1,000 investment in a five-year venture earning no profit for the first two years, and then $500 profits in each of the following three years. At a discount rate of 10 percent a year, the present value of the profit of $500 in the third year is $376 (being $500/1.10^3), $342 (being $500/1.10^4) in the fourth year and $310 (being $500/1.10^5) in the final year. Adding these cashflows (-$1,000 + $376 + $342 + $310), the venture returns the initial investment plus $28. This is the FCF value (the value) of the venture and the price that would be expected to be paid for it. As illustrated by this example, this method of valuation accommodates ventures that make large initial investments in anticipation of future profits. As a side note, an implication of this method of valuing a business on future cash flows, is that past investment in assets is irrelevant other than in the cash flow composition for today, and consequently, going forward into time.

In this setting, expected profit is the residual expected cash income after paying cash outflows. They are expected because there is uncertainty about their actual amount due to: future prices being unknown; miscalculations of the market opportunity; and organisation ability and other arrangements put in place turn out to operate differently from what was planned. Uncertainty adds cost that arise from the organisation's endeavours to ensure that its business plans are met. In this setting, uncertainty reduces business value. Uncertainty can also bring lucky breaks through identifying opportunities from which the organisation can benefit, thus increasing its value. Uncertainty is usually referred to as risk, although risk is a type of uncertainty that is amenable to statistical analysis.

An organisation's capabilities and information that increase profit compared to competitors, increases its value. Capabilities and information that achieve this are core competencies. It follows from this that core competencies are a scarce resource which on generating more profit, increase the value of the business. This method of determining the price of a scarce resource is different from how the price of other assets is determined, which is simply by demand and supply considerations (nonetheless, market value for a scarce resource can be different to the FCF value because of demand considerations). Core competencies can also increase value where they are leveraged to distend profit from existing resources, and/or extend the time horizon for profit.

Features of core competencies

The consequence of this behaviour of capabilities and supporting information created in a production process distend and/or extend profit are core competencies and are, as summarised in the VRIO model:

1. valuable;

2. rare;

3. difficult to imitate; and

4. there is the organisational ability to exploit them, whether through knowhow and the operation of organisation wide systems and processes.

Aside from generating positive value, being 'valuable' carries the requirement that core competencies align with the organisation's purpose. Where this is not the case, the organisation is better off in realising the value of the scarce resource by selling it. Rarity and the ability to imitate core competencies places them in the market to face the actions competitors can take to diminish the value of this scarce resource, and conversely actions by management to increase their value. Whereas the organisational ability gets to the heart of an organisation using core competencies. Organisations with poor organisational ability may have capabilities and information with the potential to be core competencies but lack the ability to realise their value.

Identifying a feature that may be essential to an organisation's survival does not make this a core competence. For example, electricity supply may be essential to an organisation's operations but for most organisations there is no advantage in investing in developing a core competence in electricity generation, instead, there are other considerations such as the decision to invest in standby power supply.

Formulated as a decision tree the features of core competencies is depicted in Figure 1. Supposing that the information is available, then the framework provides a visual means of assessing the potential that an organisation might have developed capabilities with supporting information that are core competencies. It has the potential because it may not actually have fully realised these competencies. By reversing the decision logic, the decision tree is useful in that it also shows what must be done to turn a poor performing capability and its supporting information into one that is a core competency.

Figure 1 *Decision tree of features of core competencies*

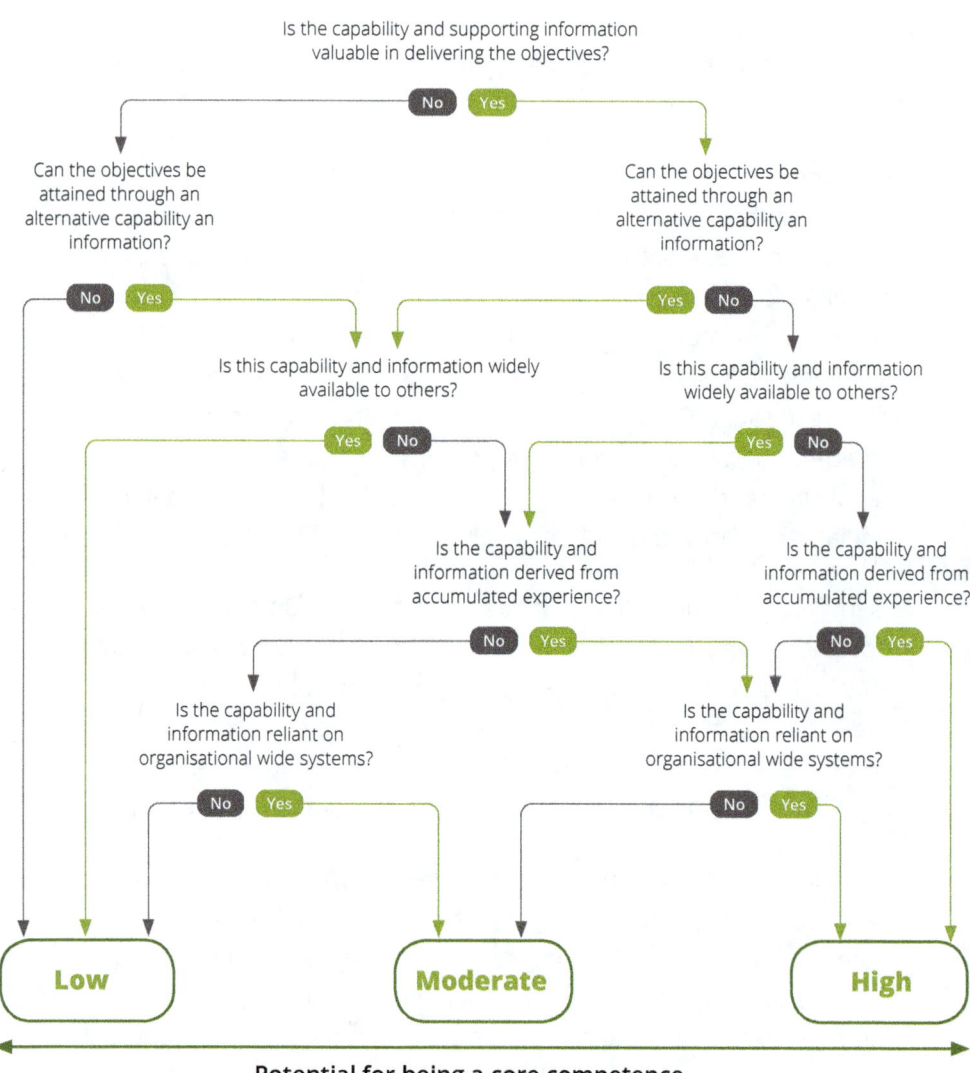

Core Competencies: Real options as corporate strategy

Core competencies can exist for each of the contributors of value

To place this in the wider context of the organisation, core competencies can be created in any of the contributors to profit, and their best use can be in any of the contributors. These contributors encompass capabilities that can extract value from markets through:

- Supply of products whose value-for-money is greater than alternatives, for example through product design and market segmentation (Contributor 1).
- Economical selection and purchase of a set of inputs to support a highly productive production process (Contributor 2).
- Operating efficient production processes (Contributor 3).
- Reliably delivering on business plans with the resilience to realise on-going profitability (Contributor 4).
- Effective establishment and management of contractual obligations (Contributor 5).

There are several ramifications for an organisation being at the nexus of many markets, orchestrating the extraction of value from each market. A key one is that all capabilities and supporting information in an organisation should be assessed in terms of the contribution it makes to improving the value of the organisation. No capability should be considered a necessary overhead that is privileged and exempt from having to show its contribution to business value.

Analysing core competencies

An exposition of core competencies must address the following questions:

- What is the business context for producing the product? Context covers the business objectives; the product and the different places being taken in the value network by buyers, competitors and suppliers; market share achieved by competitors and prices being charged, and the trends acting on the value network. Context is relevant to matters concerning core competencies because on the one hand, as the value shows, core competencies arise when an organisation produces products demanded by the market at a higher unit gross margin than competitors. On the other hand, business continuity requires that the production process must be capable of responding to the dynamics of the market.

- Who are the competitors? This information affects the scope of the description of the product, and the business angle being applied to participate in the market.
- How is the product produced? This traverses the activity type, production process, and capabilities and information of the production process. It gets to the kernel of the operational issues of the production process able to: produce products at low average unit cost; and flexibility to respond to challenges imposed by the market context in which the organisation operates.
- Why have core competencies been created? This considers the source of the value derived from the production process, for example whether due to organisation wide systems and processes and/or knowhow from accumulated experience.
- Which ways are available to imitate a core competency or sidestep the need for it, and the cost of doing that? This examines the ability to imitate the production process evaluating the alternative ways that the benefits of core competencies can be obtained, and the availability and price of those alternatives. The key attribute is the organisation's ability to reliably meet value enhancing plans in the face of the uncertain business conditions it faces. The ability to manage uncertainty is an element of possessing core competencies that are difficult to imitate, and confer competitive advantage.

- Where are the opportunities to parlay existing core competencies? The ability to continuously parlay core competencies into new opportunities is a gauge of rarity of the core competency. This is a dynamic view of core competencies – being able to continuously give effect to enhancing the value of the organisation.
- When is the occasion to parlay core competencies, create new core competencies or harvest their value? In this sense core competencies are a real option managed as part of the portfolio of salient options distending the organisation and extending its life expectancy.

An explanation of how to answer these questions is provided in the following chapters. There are chapters dealing with: the business context for leveraging core competencies; the production process being used and the source of the organisational ability to exploit core competencies. With knowledge of the core competencies of an organisation, there is discussion on the ways in which core competencies are made difficult to imitate where an organisation has developed resilience to reliably realise its business plans, and make them rare by creating real options to parlay them into new business angles.

The topic of this book is existing core competencies, or capabilities and information with the potential to be core competencies. It does not traverse other types of scarce resources, and how they can be created by an organisation. This discussion considers the supply side responses by management to maintain and improve value of the organisation and does not consider demand, other than as currently understood by the organisation and its competitors, and the expected impact of macro-trends on that position.

Chapter 1
The context for the emergence of core competencies

Organisation's objectives

Clarifying the objective in creating a production process with core competencies is always the first step in any project. The purpose covers considerations such as: aim, return, risk, resources, ongoing commitment to the organisation, fit with the available capital, and control requirements. There are many different objectives an organisation may have for their core competencies, and the following discussion assumes that core competencies are to distend and extend business value. The need for clarity on the organisation's objective comes to the fore when considering the different ways that core competencies can be used to create real options.

The business opportunity component of a business angle

A central idea behind the approach described in this book is the concept of the business angle. The business opportunity is materialised and monetarised though products. Products are exchanged between parties in the context of place in the value network, and contractual relationships bind parties in these economic transactions. The nature of this relationship is described in the product type and coordination mechanism (amongst other properties). Possible product types are: Exchange products which provide a high degree of readiness for use and transfer decision-making rights to consume or use; Interface products associated with the interaction between systems and processes, or channels for delivering exchange products; and Applications products, which extend the use of the provider's knowhow, systems and processes to new adjacent workflow processes or value networks by providing extra functionality. As an example of these types of products, the sale of gas and gas appliances to consumers are exchange products. The connection to a gas distribution network is an interface product. The annual certification of the safety of the appliances and connection are applications products.

Products are exchanged according to the coordination mechanisms used between the parties. The coordination mechanisms are: Push/pull coordination involving production for inventory, that is subsequently drawn down by buyers as used, for example, in the production of manufactured commodities; Push/push coordination occurs where the quantity supplied is determined by the volume produced and the coordination problem is solved by pricing for example, in the production of agricultural produce; Pull/push coordination provides access to on-demand production typically for combining with other products before delivery to the purchaser such as the production of a batch of printed circuit boards to be used in the assembly of an electronic device; and Pull/pull coordination is on-demand production and is used for products that are customised to the purchaser's requirements. The coordination mechanism gives effect to the product's specification and is an integral part of the production process. Production processes, and the core competencies developed, are specific to product specifications. A change to the product specification, for example, the type and required coordination mechanism, can change the supporting production process.

The value network, and macro-trends acting on it

Analysis of production processes is done in the context of the markets that make up the value network for the product, the suppliers of inputs, competitors and the other actors that shape the institutional environment in which the organisation operates. Three things are of interest, first, the competing products (their specification, price, perceived benefits and market share). Second, the different business angles being utilised to compete in the supply of the product and the inputs they use.

Third, the impact of trends on the shape and composition of the value network especially how this might impact the allocation of value added between the different parties, and therefore on the ongoing value of the business. This information provides insight into the strength of competitive advantage provided by the core competencies developed in production processes.

Value networks can change quite dramatically over a relatively short timeframe, for example, over a five year period. The extent of the change in the composition of a value network is uncovered using a value network map. A value network map provides a snapshot at a point in time of the flows in a value network in delivering products. The key participants and stages in the value network and their relative market share are depicted with customers placed on the right-hand side of the map and providers (and in turn their suppliers) on the left-hand side. The map is concerned with the allocation of value added to parties at each stage and not the flow of materials and their transformation (where information on value added is unavailable market share is used). In competitive markets it is convenient to cluster players into groups based on the similarity of competitive behaviour at each stage in the value network. At least three stages are depicted, one stage on either side of the positioning in the value network being considered. It could be more if a significant market disruption were in the offering, or a value controller is a key resource provider.

The macro-trends that influence capital flows to change the structure of the value network can be analysed in the value network map. This is done by depicting the situation today, and that expected in the foreseeable future. This analysis shows changes in players, products, and value added for each stage in the value network. Figure 2 gives an illustrative value network map for a parcel delivery service. Here there are four stages in the value network, with three alternatives for delivery: inhouse delivery, the postal network, and by a competitive market of courier companies.

The VIRO model is static, whereas markets can change rapidly. Identifying the macro-trends shaping the value network can help understand how core competencies can be expected to respond to change. Production processes need to match the dynamics of the market, and therefore, production processes must respond to the dynamism of the market or become obsolete. Figure 2 also shows a scenario for the parcel delivery sector in five years time, in which more senders outsource delivery to courier companies, and some courier companies, through vertical integration, provide contract fulfilment services. The illustrative macro-trends driving these changes are: rise of online retail supported by more parcel deliveries; and expectation by buyers of an online service experience better than that from a physical store. For courier companies, this has several implications, firstly, the growth opportunity; but to participate in this service, standards must improve to support a better customer experience, and this will involve greater use of information and integration with senders' systems. To enable this to happen, there is an opportunity to provide fulfilment services to senders.

The example in Figure 2 is a simplified business-to-business parcel delivery service, in which:

- The market today is mainly serviced by an inhouse capability, courier companies and the postal network. Many senders have their own delivery function delivering to their own customers with fulfilment from inhouse capabilities. Otherwise, senders contract with courier companies and the postal operator to do deliveries, and a significant source and destination of these parcels are from international courier companies and postal operators. Some fulfilment is contracted out to third party providers. Where outsourcing is undertaken this is by competitive contracting. International relationships are long-term bilateral agreements.
- The market is in change being driven by the rise of online retail supported by more parcel deliveries; and expectation of an online

service experience better than that in a physical store. The consequences of this are thought to be that more senders will contract with providers of delivery and fulfilment services. Some courier companies will become full-service providers supplying delivery and fulfilment services.
- A feature of this value network is the widespread use of contract owner/drivers for courier and long-haul transport. With the move to more contracting out by senders, the sector will make greater use of contract owner/drivers.

Analysis of the value network can provide the following indications of the expected nature of competing production processes:

- Production processes deliver a well-defined courier product in a highly competitive market, although opportunities for integration with fulfilment will become more evident.
- Different production processes, and activity types are being used - some organisations employing drivers, and others using contracted owner/drivers.
- Declining cost economies achieved by courier companies will become increasingly evident, increasing the market share of the most efficient courier companies. This will hasten industry consolidation, and with it, barriers to entry will increase. Despite this increase, the market will remain highly competitive.

These observations suggest that production processes used by larger courier companies are developing core competencies that provide competitive advantage.

Figure 2 *Illustrative value network map for parcel delivery services showing market share and key players at different times and the macro-trends driving change*

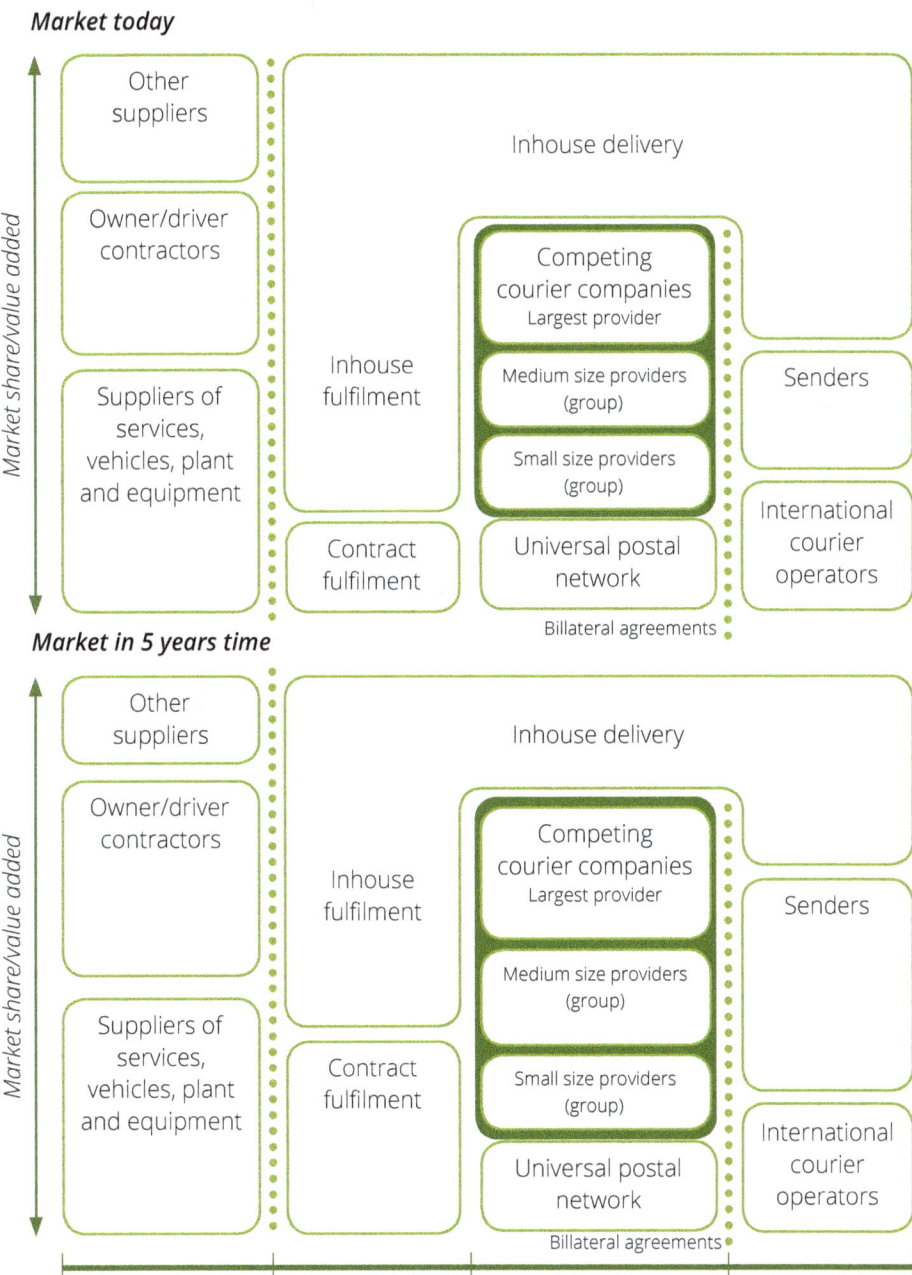

Heuristic market supply curve

A heuristic market supply curve shows the estimated costs and market shares achieved by the participants in the market compared to the price for a product. The information from the market supply curve is used to gauge the size of the relative magnitude of the value of an organisation's core competencies. In this use of the market supply curve, the relative costs structure of the participants can usually only be guessed.

In a market with many suppliers of an identical product, as a rule of thumb, market share is distributed between participants based on competitors' cost structure and capacity constraints. The proposition being that an organisation's available capacity and average unit cost sets its market share. By ordering the producers from lowest to highest average unit cost, and for each price from highest to lowest sales gives the heuristic market supply curve. The organisation with the lowest average unit cost, and therefore, highest unit gross margin has core competencies. The organisation with the highest average unit cost has no core competencies, but operates at the market price. Where a market is in change over time, as indicated by the value network map, heuristic market supply curves can be developed for each point in time.

An example of the calculation of market share is given in the table in Figure 3. In this example there are two large competitors accounting for 70 percent of market share, three medium sized competitors (18 percent market share), and a raft of small players, accounting for 12 percent of the market - where there are many small suppliers with similar cost structures because they are using the same production process, they can be classed together as a single type of competitor.

Using the assumption that market share is distributed according to average unit cost and implied resources invested (and therefore the allocation of value added), then a guess of the observed market supply curve is stepped with the competitor with largest market share on the lowest rung, the second largest competitor on the second rung and the others on the top rung. The top rung would be the observed market price of the product. At this point in the analysis no information is available on the magnitude of the costs faced by competitors – this information is estimated in later steps in the process. Using this data, an example of a heuristic market supply curve for a market with four main/ types of providers with different (guessed) average costs is shown in Figure 3.

Using this rule of thumb, the organisation with the largest, and growing market share possesses core competencies that give the whole organisation competitive advantage. Where market share is being lost, then this suggests that another organisation is gaining competitive advantage from core competencies that it is developing. Note that the implication of this assumption is that the largest supplier has the strongest case for having developed core competencies in its production process. Figure 3 provides a graphical depiction of the conclusion reached in the analysis of the value network, that the production processes used by larger courier companies are developing core competencies providing competitive advantage.

It is also assumed that where competitive markets exist, contracting for supply is more efficient than inhouse provision. This implies that there is potential growth in market size if courier companies increase the comparative value-for-money of their delivery product.

Figure 3 *Illustrative heuristic market supply curve for a competitive market with four main/types of providers with implied relative average unit costs*

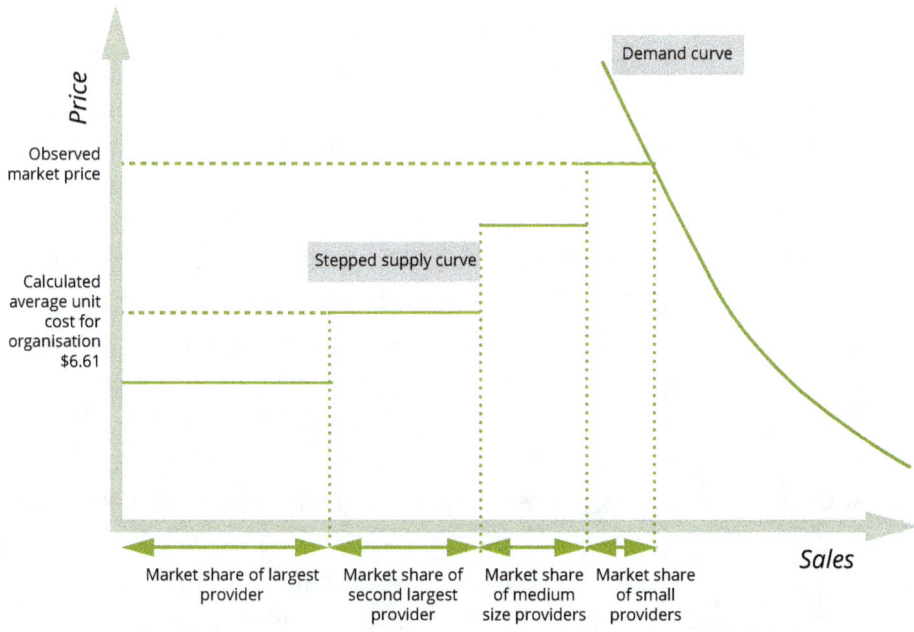

Example calculation of data used to compile the heuristic market supply curve

Providers	Market share (%)	Change in market share	Average unit cost (guessed)
Largest provider	36	Rapid growth	Lowest and much below that of small providers
Second largest provider (postal operator)	34	Slow increasing	Second lowest but close to lowest
Medium size providers (group)	18	Rapid growth	Mid
Small providers (group)	12	Small increase	Equal to market price
Total	**100**		

Average unit cost

The heuristic market supply curve shows the expected ordering of average unit cost, estimated here based on market share. The aim now is to estimate, at a high level, the average unit cost achieved by the organisation that is subject to this study, to provide a point estimate on the market supply curve. Costs in this setting are expected cash outflows incurred in operating the organisation within its life expectancy. The occurrence of cost is a function of the occurrence of planned events such as capital purchases, volume of production, rate of technical change, changes in the regulatory environment etc. Expected cash flow can, therefore, be related to these drivers of cost, in that a planned average unit cost can be calculated, which is different from the actual costs. These planned costs are:

- Variable costs, costs that change in direct proportion to change in volume. Examples are: goods for sale, contractors paid at piece rates, and energy consumed in production. The planned unit cost is the cost of a unit of output.
- Discrete costs incurred periodically. These are operating costs related to contractual commitments such as employee salaries, leases and insurance. The planned unit cost is calculated as the discreet cost included divided by planned number of units of output for that unit of input e.g. monthly salary divided by the planned number of units to be produced in a month.
- Discrete costs determined by usage, such as costs for the maintenance of plant, machinery and infrastructure. Another example is training costs to maintain the expertise of personnel that need to be periodically refreshed to avoid obsolescence. These costs exclude the cost of acquiring any assets that are maintained, but include the cost needed to maintain the planned on-going income generating ability of the asset. Planned average unit cost is calculated as the input unit cost divided by the planned number of units of output for that unit of input.

- One-off costs that are incurred, irrespective of volume. For example, capital costs incurred for the purchase of plant, machinery and infrastructure. The average unit cost falls exponentially with the volume of output produced. Planned average unit cost is calculated as cost divided by number of planned units of output before that cost is re-incurred.

An illustration of this calculation is given in Figure 4. It shows a revenue of $4,500 thousand generated on sales of 500 thousand items with no inventories - a price of $9 each. The estimated average unit cost is $6.61, and the unit profit margin is $2.59. Note that the estimate is for a point, the sales volume of 500 thousand units a year. How the average unit cost might change with different volumes is not calculated.

Figure 4 *Example of financial information used to estimate planned unit gross margin and average unit cost*

Revenue and operating expenses	Type of cost	Revenue/ cost ($'000)	Planned output (units of output for input cost)	Planned average per unit of output ($/unit output)
Gross Profit				
Revenue (annual)	Variable	4,500	500	9.00
CoGS (annual)	Variable	1,000	500	2.00
Other Operating Expenses				
Operations (per month)	Periodic	210	70 per month	3.00
Maintenance of knowhow, systems and processes	Usage	100	1,000 before service	0.10
Set-up	One-off	750	500 per production run	1.50
Insurance etc. (per month)	Periodic	5	500 per month	0.01
Average unit cost (before allowances)				6.61
Unit gross margin				29% (9.00-6.61)/9.00x100)

This information is incorporated into the heuristic market supply curve to give a fix, on the planned cost for the sales. Figure 3 shows this cost of $6.61 relative to the ranking of competitors. Using the example from the previous section, the organisation that is the largest provider is imputed to possess core competencies. If it were not the largest provider, the challenge is how to reduce average unit cost below $6.61 to create core competences.

Other than for variable costs, coinciding the timing of the incurrence of cost with the calculation period is required to ensure actual average unit cost is calculated on the same basis as planned average unit cost. Because of the differences in the timing of the incurrence and frequency/life expectancy considerations, great care is required in calculating average unit cost. For example, when working with actual cash outflows, it is crucial that expenditure on maintenance is consistent with the planned life expectancy of discrete cost items. It is common to encounter underinvestment in the maintenance of these items, and therefore, calculated actual costs being too low.

Gross margin and the wider definition of competing products

The discussion up to this point has assumed that competing products offer similar perceived benefits, and therefore, comparison of average unit cost indicates the more efficient producer. A common situation is that products with different perceived benefits vie for sales. In that situation superior unit gross margin indicates the existence and strength of organisational wide core competencies in that market. Gross margin is profit to sales revenue *(Profit/Sales)* expressed as a percentage.

Where competitors offer products with different perceived benefits and price, then this must be incorporated into the analysis. For this the value-for-money indifference, demand and market supply curves are used. An example of these curves is shown in Figure 5. The value-for-money indifference curve describes the relationship between price and the perceived benefit of the product.

Demand curves show the relationship between price and sales. Despite this relationship, the only thing known about the shape of the demand curve is the point estimate of observed prices and sales. Where competing products have quite different perceived benefits, as is shown in the diagram, those benefits are depicted in different demand curves, with the high benefit demand curve shifted to the right.

The information on the unit gross margin is used to estimate the heuristic market supply curve. Keeping with the method described earlier, this is done by first constructing the market supply curve for the lowest priced product, starting with the competitor with the greatest margin. To this is added the sales of the next largest unit gross margin product, and so on until all competitors supplying products with the same perceived benefit are incorporated into the heuristics supply curve. To these sales are then added the sales of the next largest benefit product, starting with the largest unit gross margin provider and finishing with the smallest unit gross margin provider. This process is followed until all suppliers are incorporated into the heuristic market supply curve. Where this information is unavailable, estimated market share, as described above, is used.

These three curves provide insight into which of the competitors possesses core competencies and the degree of competitive advantage this gives. Core competencies are possessed by the competitor that has the highest unit gross margin for supplying the perceived benefit of the product. If the unit gross margin is lower than that achieved by lower perceived benefit products, then the strength of that competitive advantage is broader in scope. A business's value increases as the unit gross margin increases.

Understanding how products with different benefits are competing for sales provides further information on the strength of the competitive advantage conferred by the different products, and their supporting production processes, and the business angles being followed. To illustrate this Figure 5 shows a high benefit product being sold at the price of the low benefit product. This product is preferred by buyers and will displace the low value product, and total sales will increase from 50 to 60 units. This example also illustrates how the introduction of a higher value-for-money product creates opportunities to promote economies of scale, a topic that will be returned to later.

Figure 5 *Value-for-money indifference, demand and market supply curves for products with different perceived benefits*

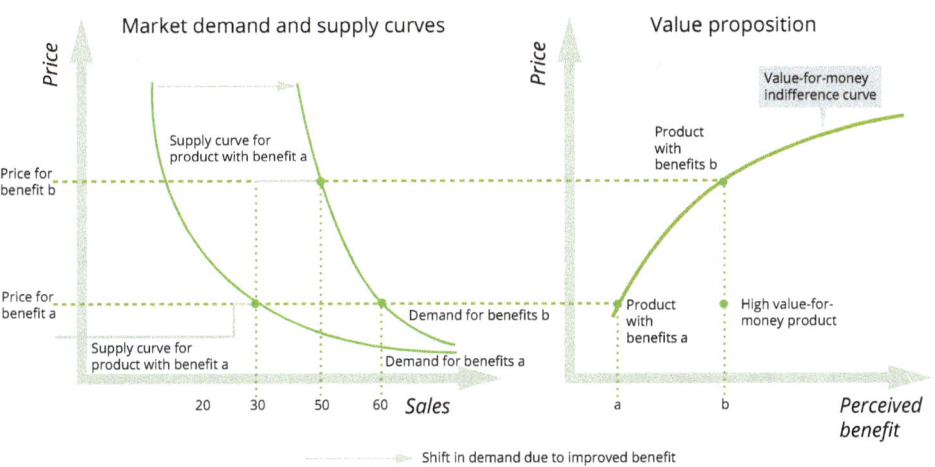

Note to figure: this depiction assumes inelastic price elasticity of demand.

The importance of economising

For organisations with sales that are much greater than price, then reducing costs is the single most effective way to increase profit. This is because, a small decrease in costs increases profits more than that achieved by a small increase in sales. For organisations involved in few high priced sales the converse is true. Organisations should usually prioritise economising when confronted with the choice between reducing costs and increasing sales in competitive markets.

Production process fits the context

In a market with many competing suppliers of a product we can talk about organisations having different potentials of possessing core competencies. Organisations with low average unit cost have high potential of possessing core competencies. Conversely, organisations with high average unit costs have low potential for core competencies. Organisations between these two ends have some potential of possessing some capabilities and information that are core competencies. This scale is fungible and depends on the organisation's average unit cost compared to the least average unit cost producer. Where a broad definition of the perceived benefit of competing products is taken, then correlations of based on unit gross margin rather than average unit costs.

A business angle consists of a perceived business opportunity and an activity type, and these are manifested in the product and its production process to exploit it. To warrant the allocation of resources, a business angle must contribute to delivering the organisation's objectives. While an organisation can have a myriad of objectives, here, the measurement of its contribution is value. The implication of this is that organisations must concentrate on creating processes that contribute value.

Production processes produce products whose specifications include their ability to conform to the economic relationships governing exchanges between parties that have dimensions of product type, coordination mechanisms, and frequency (amongst other properties). Market requirements change over time, for example due to competitor behaviour, and product specifications must change to remain relevant to buyers. To respond to this change organisations find ways to ensure that appropriate production processes are in place to enable ongoing survival. This may require changes to the production process.

A consequence of this is that to maintain business value requires continually aligning the fit between the planned position in the market and the production processes of the organisation. The continual need to respond to changes in the market recognises that the value of core competencies is determined in the market, with actions by competitors able to diminish their value, and actions by management to respond to increase their value. Where this can be achieved, the core competencies developed in the production process confer competitive advantage.

Chapter 2
Characteristics of production processes

Activity type, the other component of a business angle

Organisations choose an activity type to exploit a business opportunity, and use production processes to deliver products that meet both the objectives and constraints of the organisation, and the dynamic characteristics of the market. A production process has organisational structure, activity type consisting of a set of capabilities with supporting information, that use production technology with appropriate knowhow, systems and processes, resources, and contractual relationships to transform inputs into specified delivered products. Our interest is now to describe the production process. The first step in the analytical process is to identify the activity type being used to give effect to the business angle.

An activity type consists of methods to deliver products, and acquire inputs. The activity type matrix summarises the range of quite different activity types available to pursue a business opportunity. Four methods are used for acquisition, and four for delivery giving 16 distinct activity types. The taxonomy of activity types is given in Figure 6. A method requires systems and processes to be put in place, and these are designed to meet the requirements of the business angle. The generic methods are: Assemble, Assign, Aggregate, and Arbitrage.

Assemble delivery method produces products that provide a high degree of readiness for use – exchange and capacity products. These products can be delivered by: activity type a (Producer) using the assemble acquisition method; activity type e (Systems Integrator) using the assign acquisition method; activity type i (Supplier Cooperative) using the aggregate acquisition method; and activity type m (Assembler) using the arbitrage acquisition method.

Assign delivery method provides the capacity to operate a capability enabling organisations to contract-out part of the risk in producing outputs. The form of these example products are: exchange and capacity products. Delivery of products can be by: activity type c (Network Operator) using the assemble acquisition method; activity type g (Consolidator) using the assign acquisition method; activity type k (Insurer) using the aggregate acquisition method; and activity type o (Aggregator) using the arbitrage acquisition method.

Aggregate delivery method provides network and risk sharing products of a capacity nature which can be delivered by: activity type (p. Trader) using the assemble acquisition method; activity type l (Auctioneer) using the assign acquisition method; activity type h (Agent) using the aggregate acquisition method; and activity type d (Developer) using the arbitrage acquisition method.

Arbitrage delivery method provides products that exploit asymmetries in information and high transaction cost. The form of the products are: exchange, capability and capacity products delivered by: activity type b (Outsource Provider) using the assemble acquisition method; activity type f (Lead Contractor) using the assign acquisition method; activity type j (Underwriter) using the aggregate acquisition method; and activity type n (Broker) using the arbitrage acquisition method.

Figure 6 *Activity type matrix with description of products produced and associated sources of declining cost economies*

Guide to symbols:	Assembly	 Assign	Aggregate	 Arbitrage
Method of acquiring inputs	\multicolumn{4}{c}{Method of delivering outputs}
	a. Producer Production of products by using inputs that require significant processing. Exploiting declining cost economies that derive from scale and scope to deliver products, and on the inputs used.	**b. Outsource supplier** Supply of capacity based on utilising inputs that require significant pre-processing. Exploiting the ability to align the interests between buyer and the provider, and declining cost economies that derive from scale and scope on the inputs used.	**c. Network operator** Construction of a portfolio of purchasers of products that utilise inputs requiring significant transformation. Exploiting the law of large numbers and scale-free infrastructure networks to deliver products to buyers, and declining cost economies that derive from scale and scope on the inputs used.	**d. Developer** Resale of products derived from inputs requiring significant preparation. Exploiting price differences by utilising asymmetries in access to information and high transaction costs faced by buyers, and declining cost economies that derive from scale and scope on the inputs used.
	e. Systems integrator Production of products utilising contracted operational capacity from third parties. Exploiting declining cost economies that derive from scale and scope to deliver products, and the ability to align the interests between the provider and their suppliers to acquire inputs.	**f. Lead contractor** Supply of capacity by utilising contracted operational capacity from third parties. Exploiting the ability to align the interests between buyers and the provider, and between the provider and their suppliers.	**g. Consolidator** Construction of a portfolio of purchasers of products supplied from operational capacity contracted from third parties. Exploiting the law of large numbers and scale-free infrastructure networks to deliver products to buyers, and the ability to align the interests between the provider and their suppliers.	**h. Agent** Resale of contracted operational capacity from third parties. Exploiting price differences by utilising asymmetries in access to information and high transaction costs faced by buyers, and the ability to align the interests between the provider and their suppliers.

Method of acquiring inputs	Method of delivering outputs			
	i. Supplier cooperative Production of products by engaging with a portfolio of input suppliers. Exploiting declining cost economies that derive from scale and scope to deliver products, and law of large numbers and scale-free infrastructure networks to acquire inputs from suppliers.	**j. Underwriter** Supply of capacity by using capacity syndicated to several suppliers. Exploiting the ability to align the interests between buyers and the provider, and law of large numbers and scale-free infrastructure networks to acquire inputs from suppliers.	**k. Insurer** Construction of a portfolio of purchasers of products that is syndicated to a portfolio of suppliers. Exploiting the law of large numbers and scale-free infrastructure networks to deliver products to buyers and acquire inputs from suppliers.	**l. Auctioneer** Resale of products acquired from a range of input suppliers. Exploiting price differences by utilising asymmetries in access to information and high transaction costs faced by buyers, and law of large numbers and scale-free infrastructure networks to acquire inputs from suppliers.
	m. Assembler Production of products based on bought in sub-assembly componentry. Exploiting declining cost economies that derive from scale and scope to deliver products and price differences by utilising asymmetries in access to information, and high transaction costs faced by suppliers.	**n. Broker** Supply of capacity by on-selling capacity from suppliers. Exploiting the ability to align the interests between buyers and the provider, price differences by utilising asymmetries in access to information and high transaction costs faced by the provider and their suppliers.	**o. Aggregator** Construction of a portfolio of purchasers for products acquired for reselling. Exploiting the law of large numbers and scale-free infrastructure networks to deliver products to buyers, price differences by utilising asymmetries in access to information and high transaction costs faced by providers and their suppliers.	**p. Trader** Trading in products. Exploiting price differences by utilising asymmetries in access to information, and high transaction costs faced by buyers and suppliers.

The activity type being used by an organisation can be located on the activity type matrix by answering the questions in Figure 7. Returning to the parcel delivery service, as summarised in the value chain in Figure 2, the courier organisation used in the example provides a national delivery service through a network of contract drivers. Affirmative answers are therefore given to the questions:

- Does the production process being used in delivering outputs depend on aggregation due to benefits from the law of large numbers, or access to a network?; and
- Does the production process being used in acquiring inputs by contracting for capacity?

indicating that the organisation is operating an aggregate-assign (g. consolidator) activity type. In contrast the postal operator employing its own staff would answer affirmatively to:

- Does the production process being used in delivering outputs depend on aggregation due to benefits from the law of large numbers, or access to a network?; and
- Does the production process being used in acquiring inputs through buying or hiring components or labour?

indicating the use of the aggregate-assemble (c. network operator) activity type.

Most organisations with core competencies have a dominant activity type, getting the potential benefit of at least one source of declining cost economy in each of the delivery and acquisition methods, and use minor activity types alongside it. Hybrid activity types exploiting multiple sources of declining cost economies are also found, for example in some multisided platform organisations. The absence of a consistent activity type being used to drive declining cost economies suggest low potential for the existence of core competencies within that organisation.

Figure 7 *Questions to establish candidate delivery and acquisition methods*

Does the production process being used in...		Then it is:
... delivering outputs:	Facilitate getting other products?	■● ▲✗
	Depend on aggregation due to benefits from the law of large numbers, or access to a network?	✣
	Provide access to capacity?	✣
	Make a new product distinguishable from its component parts?	⊕
... acquiring inputs:	That are to be on-sold?	■● ▲✗
	By passing risk to a third party	✣
	By contracting for capacity?	✣
	Through buying or hiring components or labour?	⊕

Different production processes have different characteristics

An activity type uses systems and processes that are appropriate to the method, and these are components of the production process. There are distinct types of systems and processes, and each has different operational features. Systems and processes operate effectively and efficiently within a narrow band of these. To illustrate this, five operations processes employed by the assemble method are used. These five have been chosen because they are widely used, distinct, and exploit economies of scale to different degrees, and have different operational features. Operating systems and processes outside their set of operational traits renders them ineffective and inefficient. An organisation uses several systems and processes and the possibility for sub-optimal performance exists in each of these. The five assemble method operations processes used to demonstrate this point are:

- Project processes provide the capability to solve a unique set of coordination requirements involving skills, materials, budget and time to deliver a highly customised output. However, there is minimal benefit from declining cost economies. This process is found in one-off project initiatives, and research and development endeavours.
- Workshop processes undertake a variety of work that fit within its capability and capacity. Declining cost economies are from learning. Workshop processes are commonly found in maintenance and repair, and customised production such as that by professionals.
- Batch processes seek declining cost economies through standardised product specifications and are used where flexibility is needed to meet market demand for high product variety and/or small production runs. This process is widely operated, from accounts receivable and payable processing through to manufacturing.
- Line processes are characterised by economies of declining cost, derived from scale of operation, standardisation of process, with some limited flexibility for changes in product specification. Line processes are used in large scale manufacturing such as food, electronics, motor vehicles, logistics and mortgage processing.
- Continuous processes realise economies from declining cost economies derived from a limited range of highly standardised products, processed continuously to a very tight specification. Continuous processes are commonly used in chemical and ingredient manufacture, and data processing.

The comparative operational features of these production processes are set out in Figure 8. An observation from the table is that the five processes are not simply a spectrum of capabilities to produce different levels of output, rather each is designed to meet the characteristics of demand being targeted by the organisation.

While five assemble delivery method operations processes are described here, a wide range of other operations processes exist to provide different sets of traits, and to exploit different sources of declining cost economies. For example, three commonly used processes used by the aggregate method are based on point-to-point, hub-and-spokes, and point-to-multipoint networks that exploit scale free network economies, and these networks are supported by different sort methods such as hierarchy, sequence and attribute sort which give different levels of benefit from the law of large numbers.

Figure 8 *Comparative operational features of five types of assemble delivery method operations processes*

Operational features	Operations process				
	Project	Workshop	Batch	Line	Continuous
Capacity definition	◀ HIGH DIVERSITY				FIXED ONCE SET ▶
Set-up costs to change	◀ VARIABLE	LOW			HIGH ▶
Volume	◀ ONE-OFF				HIGH ▶
Change in capacity	VARIABLE	RESOURCING	PROCESS	PROCESS	FACILITY
Asset specificity	VARIABLE	HIGH	◀ LOW		HIGH ▶
Knowledge of operations tasks	VARIABLE	KNOWN BUT OFTEN NOT WELL DEFINED	WELL DEFINED		
Knowledge of materials requirements	KNOWN AT SPECIFICATION STAGE	SOME UNCERTAINTY	KNOWN		
Material handling logistics	VARIABLE	◀ LOW			HIGH ▶
Span of knowhow	◀ WIDE	SOME			LIMITED ▶
Control of operations	◀ COMPLEX				PRESCRIBED ▶
Control of quality	PERIODIC	AD HOC	DESIGNED INTO PROCESS		
Unit process time	◀ LONG				SHORT ▶
Ability to control delivery time/cost	◀ DIFFICULT				EASY ▶
Nature & place of bottlenecks	◀ FREQUENT AND MOVABLE			FEW, KNOWN AND FIXED ▶	
Impact of breakdown	◀ LOW				HIGH ▶
Market coordination mechanism	PULL		PUSH		
Flexibility to accommodate changes	◀ FLEXIBLE				INFLEXIBLE ▶
Precision of coordination	HIGH	◀ LOW			HIGH ▶
Ability to deal with ad hoc coordination problems once in operation	◀ HIGH				LOW ▶
Orientation of innovation	RISK	SKILL	PRODUCT	PROCESS	PROCESS
Uncertainty once in operation	◀ HIGH				LOW ▶

The operational features have business implications in terms of what the production process can do and how it behaves. For example, the project process can fabricate one-off custom design products, whereas this is not possible using a continuous process which is designed to produce high volumes of products with little variation in specification. Each has a different set of business implications, therefore they are not substituting for one another, but are quite different in their application. Figure 9 gives more examples of how the business implications of these five operations processes are different.

Figure 9 *Business implications of five assemble delivery method operations processes*

Business implications	Production process				
	Project	Workshop	Batch	Line	Continuous
Product	CAN BE DIFFICULT TO SPECIFY		DETAILED SPECIFICATION WITH TOLERANCES		
Basis of product	CAPABILITY	CAPABILITY	STANDARDISED PRODUCT		
Product variety	HIGH DIVERSITY		STANDARD		
Order size	ONE-OFF				LARGE ▶
Variation accommodated	◀ HIGH				NONE ▶
Market coordination mechanism	UNIQUE CONTRACT		STANDARDISED CONTRACT		
Organisational control	DECENTRALISED		CENTRALISED		
Organisational style	ENTREPRENEURIAL		BUREAUCRATIC		
Unit of accountability	PROJECT		OUTPUT		
Dominant operations perspective	SKILL & EXPERIENCE		PRESCRIBED		
Nature of skill or knowhow	ACCUMULATED EXPERIENCE		ORGANISATIONAL WIDE SYSTEMS		
Input specification	SPECIFIC TO PROJECT		DETAILED SPECIFICATION WITH TOLERANCES		
Fixed assets	VARIABLE	◀ LOW			HIGH ▶
Opportunities for declining cost economies	◀ LOW				HIGH ▶
Raw material inventories	AS REQUIRED		PLANNED WITH SAFETY STOCK		
Work-in-progress	◀ HIGH				LOW ▶
Finished goods inventories (depends on the coordination method used)	◀ NONE				HIGH ▶
Material costs	RELATIVELY HIGH				RELATIVELY LOW
Labour cost	RELATIVELY HIGH				RELATIVELY LOW

The description of different types of processes is in terms of operational features, and the business implications of these. These are technical characteristics. In contrast to this, the business requirements on an organisation are for attributes such as consumer experience, product functional specification, perceived value-for-money, ascribed product meaning, brand association etc. A process is chosen whose business implications best fit the desired business requirements. There will be an imperfect match. This is because a process obeys scientific laws, and technical and engineering constraints. This means that an organisation gerrymanders a process to fit its business requirements. This leads to two problems: first, to achieve a fit the process can be used in an inefficient way and fixes can be costly; and second, there are limitations to the degree to which a process can cope with changes in business requirements, which in turn need to respond to changes that occur over time in the market.

For core competencies, processes are operated to make best use of their technical characteristics. Determining whether a production process is operated in a manner consistent with its technical characteristics is done by assessing the degree to which it aligns with the operational and business characteristics described in Figure 8 and Figure 9. The resultant profile shows how a process is being used in practice, compared to the technical features that stem from its design. A process with inconsistent attributes is evidence that the capabilities and information involved in the production process have low potential of being core competencies. Inconsistency in production processes frequently arise because an organisation has a lack of expertise about production processes and have underinvested in it. Organisations operating inconsistent production processes are unsustainable because they are unable to achieve low average unit costs

Capabilities of the organisational wide systems and processes

A method consists of the functional binary of operational management to operate (1) delivery/acquisition processes, and (2) marketing and sales processes. These two functions are of equal importance. This binary is most obvious for the product delivery method. The production process used in a method is made up of a set of capabilities and supporting information. A capability with its information is the capacity provided by knowhow, systems and processes to perform functional actions such as to deliver specified products, to execute risk mitigation actions to ensure business plans are realised, and to undertake actions to secure scarce resources by maintaining and enhancing their on-going income earning ability.

A high-level depiction of some capabilities and information flows for a simple parcel courier enterprise utilising the aggregate-assign activity type is presented in Figure 10. The analysis should be at a sufficiently high-level to enable a meaningful understanding of the functions to perform a production process. A capability may have no employees to undertake the work, as it may be fully automated. The diagram shows:

- Marketing and sales capabilities primary from a Sales and Customer Relationship capability with active involvements of the Leadership, Strategy and Communications capability for the management of major accounts.
- Most of the capabilities are involved with the operations of providing a courier service.
- The main input is finding and contracting for drivers, and there is a capability dedicated to this.
- There is risk and business continuity management provided by the Leadership, Strategy and Communications capability, and Finance and Compliance capability.

As a side note, organisational structure determines the functional actions carried out by an organisation, and the ways in which these are performed, and relate to one another. Figure 10 embodies a functional organisational structure that operates each capability as a distinct management unit with formal communications between each unit. An organisational architecture that uses collaborative working practices and information sharing would have information flows to reflect those relationships, and would be different from those shown in Figure 10.

Figure 10 *Capabilities and information flow diagram for a parcel delivery service using the aggregate-assign activity type*

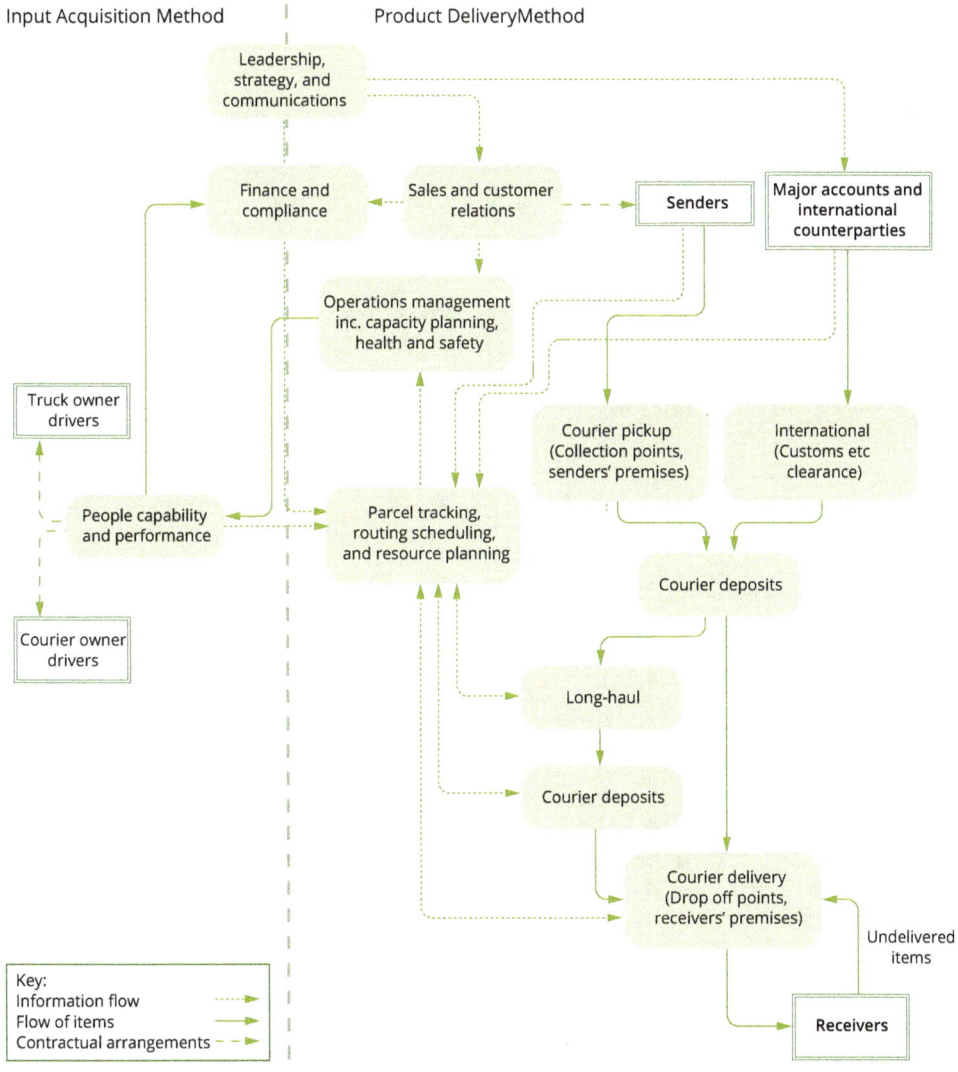

In this discussion of core competencies, an immediate question that arises is whether the set of capabilities and information flows depicted in Figure 10 are appropriate for the chosen production process. One technique to answer this question is to compare the capabilities to a hypothesised ideal process. This type of comparison is shown in Figure 11. The example given is the operations process component of the delivery method capabilities used by a process producing statistical information. The diagram shows the ideal process operating with a full set of capabilities, and the actual process with deficiencies in its capabilities - indicated by the ghosted capabilities and absent information flows.

Figure 11 *Comparison of some operations process capabilities used in the production of statistical information against a hypothesised ideal process*

Ideal statistical process

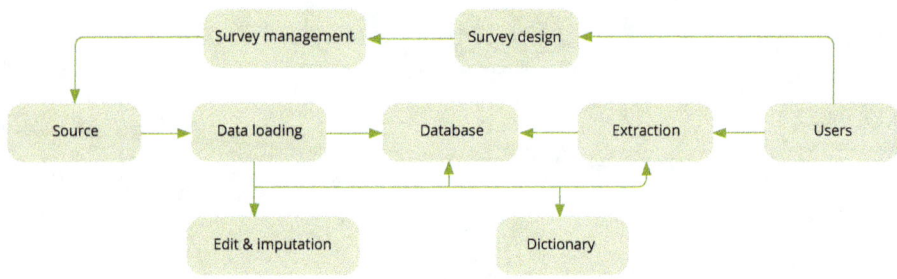

Actual process in use

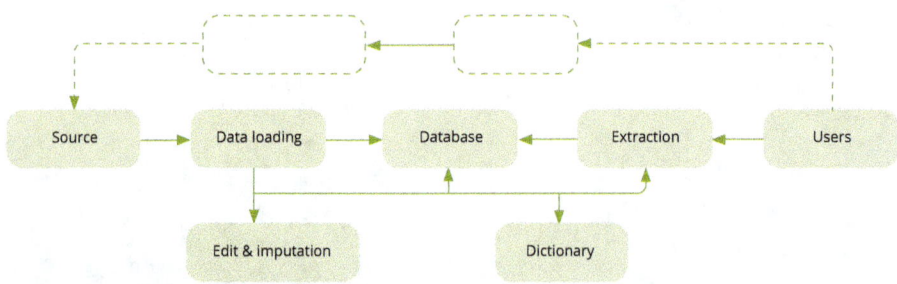

Organisational ability provided by expertise

To specify a hypothetical ideal set of capabilities for a production process requires expertise and experience. Knowhow is the domain specific expertise and experience that is applied to specified capabilities to profit from scarce resources and speculation. People with knowhow are both profit producers and knowledge contributors, and their abilities are judged by the organisation's performance in the market. This is a high bar, and there are two issues concerning the state of knowhow in an organisation, the first is whether it can deliver this outcome (reliably 'walk the talk' to achieve high business value), or whether it is confined to just using the language of business ('all talk'). The second, is the degree of interaction with other knowledge domains to make value adding business decisions.

A decision tree to establish the state of expertise of a person or group of people to provide the performance required of a capability is given in Figure 12. The state of expertise for a core competence must contribute to profit. This requires the ability to reliably formulate solutions by doing complex calculations in a wide variety of applications within the domain, explain the choice of calculation to arrive at that solution, and reliably execute those solutions. To work with other capabilities there needs to be interactional expertise as well – this is a lower level of expertise that enables domains to work together, and requires a level of understanding of that other domain. To be effective, interactional expertise, nonetheless, requires a level of expertise in that other domain, such as, to routinely do simple calculations (apply 'rules of thumb') from that other domain. In contrast to this, where simple buying decisions are being made, primary source knowledge may be enough.

Different knowledge domains have different ways to test its veracity, and its reliability to contribute to business value. Scientific expertise is tested through peer review processes, technology through its useful application, operations management through the efficiency of the production process, product design by adoption by users, and artistic endeavours by the commentary from critics and consumers.

The development of interactional expertise about another domain does not make the person a contributor expert with knowhow in that other domain. If a person or group of people are to reliably contribute to the development and maintenance of core competencies it is imperative that there is a realistic appreciation of the level of expertise available to an organisation. It is easy for people that do not possess knowhow, repeatedly tested as evidenced by a track record of creating and maintaining core competencies in a wide range of settings, to overestimate their expertise. This is the phenomenon of knowledge illusion – here Alexander Pope's warning is worth remembering 'A little learning is a dangerous thing; Drink deep, or taste not the Pierian spring: There shallow draughts intoxicate the brain, And drinking largely sobers us again.' (from An Essay on Criticism published in 1711).

Overestimation of the level of expertise is commonly found in organisations not subject to strong competitive pressures, or whose production processes have weak potential of having developed core competencies. In these types of settings, self-defined performance assessment is commonly advanced as the evidence of claimed high level of expertise. This is frequently accompanied by narrowed codification of expertise, and a history of poor investment in analytical and evaluation capabilities. A reputation of being a 'safe pair of hands' to reliably get things done to address straightforward, first order business needs does not provide evidence of knowhow capable of creating core competencies. Overestimating the level of expertise increases the risk faced by an organisation, as well as reducing the potential to build core competencies.

Figure 12 *Decision tree to establish state of expertise*

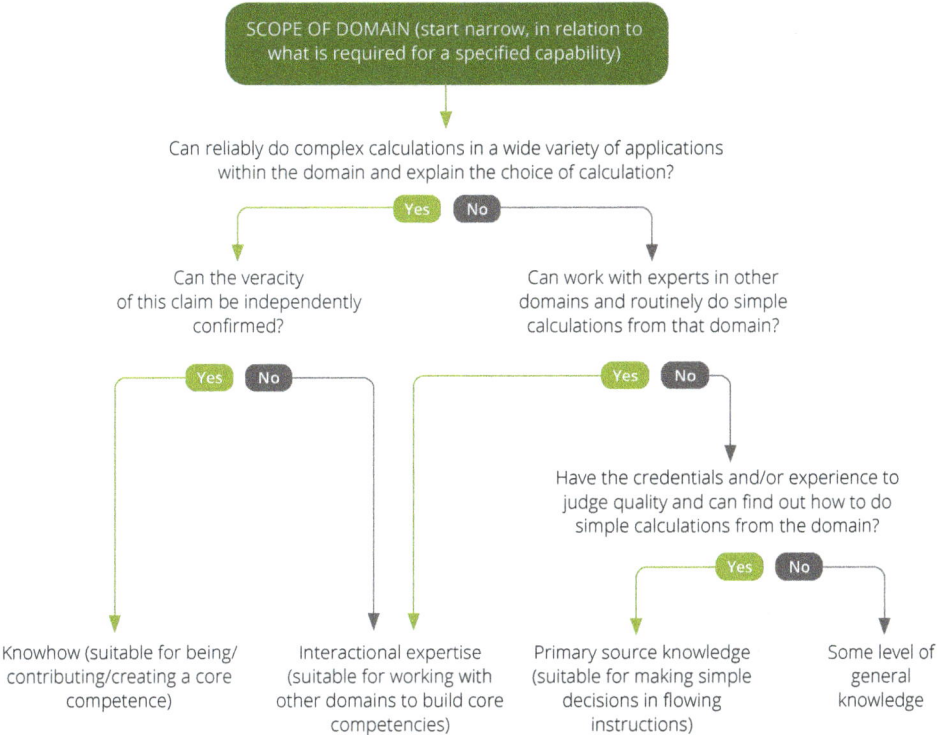

An illustration of the scope of interaction between four knowledge domains that might be found in an organisation is depicted in Figure 13. A circle represents a distinct domain of expertise about a capability. A triangle indicates the interaction between two domains. The apex of the triangle indicates the domain with an interest in the domain at the base of the triangle. The length of the base indicates the breath of the interest in that domain. An overlap between the interest of two domains indicates a cross flow of ideas which contribute to the development of domain knowledge. For example, to create business value operations managers and product designers must collaborate on equal terms, frequently, possessing a high level of shared understanding, and pursuing a common objective. Operations managers need to understand product design enough to make products to specification, and with the desired product lifespan. Similarly, product designers must design products that can be made profitably. Each should possess contributor expertise though proficiency in a set of practices, and fluency in the language that describes practices in collaborating with other domains, without proficiency in them in the form of interactional expertise.

Both operations managers and product designers interact with customers, operations managers to minimise whole of life costs, and product designers to develop high value-for-money products to support the organisation's product positioning strategy, for example. For operations managers this is in terms of metrics such as mean time before failure, time to respond to service requests, cost of product failure, cost to improve quality. For product designers, a product can be judged from benefits derived from its functional attributes as well as its aesthetic benefits. Here, because of the commercial impact of market feedback effects, such as word-of-mouth, the license to judge the output of product design can extend beyond verification of functional claims to include evaluations from other stakeholders such as the public (e.g. experience of everyday life), critics, advocacy groups (e.g. animal welfare) and government agencies (e.g. health and safety, and emission standards). The breadth of evaluation is much broader and the tensions between the evaluations by different stakeholders more difficult to balance. Product designers may consider they have a refined sense of aesthetics, as other specialist have in their own fields, but this counts for nothing where this fails to advance the objectives of an organisation. The collaboration between operations manager and product designers from the development of interactional expertise between two domains can fertilise innovation in the associated contributor expertise.

Business leadership must marshal a range of domain knowledges and for this interactional expertise is required. The level of interactional expertise in each domain will depend on the pressures on the organisation and its core competencies. The level of interactional expertise needs to be extensive, and may need to be rooted in knowhow in the domain of the core competence. From the point of view that profit is derived from core competencies and speculation, business leadership that is devoid of interactional expertise is naive speculation. It is a mistake to think that there is such a capability as a universal, general-purpose leader who can be parachuted into any situation. Indeed, in some settings, contributor expertise in the domain of the core competencies may be a prerequisite for a leader.

Figure 13 *Illustration of scope of interaction between four knowledge domains*

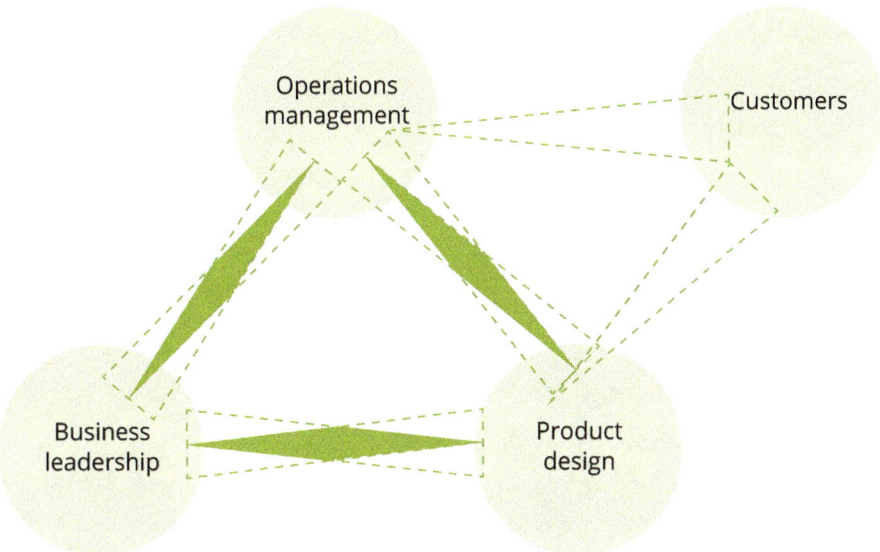

Driving declining cost economies in organisational wide systems and processes

For a given product, the profile of the mix of one-off, variable, periodic discrete, and usage based costs is determined by the production process. Organisational ability activates on one or more drivers of declining cost economies fostering core competencies that result in the organisation achieving a lower average unit cost than those of competitors. Declining cost economies can impact each of the categories of cost. The drivers of declining cost economies are:

- Economies of scale.
- Alignment of the interests of the parties to a transaction.
- The law of large numbers.
- Economies from aggregation.
- Information asymmetries.

Economies of scale

Economies of scale due to increase in volume of output leading to the reduction in average unit cost. Reasons for this are:

- High capital investment, which in some settings can fall exponentially with increased use.
- High set-up costs (for example, faced by software developers in developing applications programs), which can fall exponentially with number of uses.
- Opportunities for process improvement (reduced variation) and simplification.
- Learning from repetition.
- Speed of operation that increases with volume.
- Physical relationship between area (which increases at the square) and volume (which increases at the cube) in pipes and containers.
- Procurement where volume discounts are available.
- Access to better managerial and technical skills.

The last two benefits can also be realised because the organisation is bigger, giving rise to economies of size. As an example, a large organisation with a large spend on advertising can negotiate lower prices. Related are economies of scope where, more product variety gives rise to economies of scope. For example, distribution channels are better utilised with the addition of similar products.

Alignment of the interests of the parties to a transaction

Incentives and sanctions, close monitoring and formal contracts are among the ways of aligning the interests of the parties involved in the transaction. Each of these ways imposes costs (called agency costs) on the parties. Agency costs rise the more the interests of the parties diverge. Outsourcing a capability and buying in a product is generally more efficient than internal supply when:

- the buyer can monitor the performance of external suppliers;
- the cost of measuring supplier performance is not out of proportion to the product's purchase price;
- the cost of the risk of performance failure by the supplier is low; and
- there is no requirement on the part of the supplier to make large investment in contract specific personnel, systems and processes, and other relationship specific assets to deliver the product.

The law of large numbers

The law of large numbers applies where, with more occurrences of an unconnected event (motor accidents while driving on an open road for example), the occurrence of an event (an accident) lies more closely to the average occurrence of the event (say, one accident every 10,000 hours of driving). Statistical techniques are used to measure and analyse the characteristics of these occurrences. The law of large numbers arises in a wide range of settings: sorts (e.g. mail and parcels), searches (e.g. internet queries), queues (e.g. incoming telephone calls), selection (e.g. purchase of products), data analysis (e.g. weather forecasting), and accidents and errors (e.g. motor vehicle accidents).

Economies from aggregation

Cost savings from aggregation can also come from clustering of buyers and suppliers near one another in a geographic location. Cost reductions can be achieved from the design of hub-and-spokes in infrastructure networks. Scale-free infrastructure network architectures exploit the relationship that, in hub-and-spoke networks, costs increase linearly with the number of connections to a spoke, whereas those for point-to-point networks increase at the square. Network architecture is relevant to utilities, logistic delivery, and distributed computing networks.

Information asymmetries

Information asymmetries arise where it is costly to acquire information. While it can be costly to obtain, information once gained, all subsequent uses of the information are at no additional cost. Once gained the average unit cost of acquiring the information falls exponentially with use. Uncertainty can also impose cost. One example is the aptly called cost of 'lemons' where it is difficult to detect a defective product before purchase. The possibility of buying a lemon reduces the price of good products. Order cost is a type of transaction cost sustained to discover new information. Information about the identity of suppliers, establish a relationship with a supplier, to place an order, to arrange shipping, shipping, handling on arrival and unpacking, evaluate the quality of the product and reliability of the supplier. Consideration of order costs applies where inventories are involved because they can determine the economic order quantity - economic order quantity is a function of demand, order costs and holding costs. The nature of this relationship is such that as order costs fall, economic order size falls more rapidly (at the square root).

Planned average unit cost and capacity

With knowledge of the competing products (how they are positioned in the value for money map and demand), an organisation can plan to invest to be the lowest average unit cost producer. This is a strategy that can be used where the planned production process has strong declining cost economies. At its essence, this strategy is to price at a level that will give the planned market share – a volume where the organisation is profitable at the planned level of production. Organisations, in planning the returns from investment may be prepared to make substantial initial investment with no profit for a period before becoming profitable. Organisations can plan to disrupt a market and become the major player by investing in capacity that achieves economies of scale at levels greater than that achieved by other players by pricing at a level supported by a low planned average unit cost. The initial demand to gain the benefits of declining costs from scale can be underwritten by the organisation's own needs, or foundation/government procurement contracts.

Organisations that aim to be amongst the largest (three, for example) players in a sector, may indirectly be pursuing strategies to strengthen core competencies created in the production process. But this may not always be the case, because this objective is a statement only about market share. It says nothing about the business angle - that would require the stated objective to say something about the production process, such as what declining cost economies are to be exploited to achieve this market share.

Core competencies give value to a business angle

Profit is derived from production processes to successfully speculate, and reliably supply products at low average unit cost. In a market, different production processes give effect to the different activity types that compete with one another for a share of the available value added. A production process has organisational structure, activity type consisting of a collection of capabilities and information that use production technology. Production processes are categorised by their technical attributes, and these in turn have different business features. Technical attributes are quite different from business requirements, which are for attributes such as consumer experience, product functional specification, perceived value-for-money, ascribed product meaning, brand association etc. A production process must be engineered to give results that yield the business requirements. Compromises are made, as well as rectifying these to deliver the required business requirements, and this adds cost, but the payback is from improved business value.

Cost of compromise is different from the increased costs imposed by: misalignment in the activity type; deficiencies in capabilities and their information; inappropriate production processes; failure to realise declining cost economies; and ignorance. These shortcomings in the production process are prima facie evidence that the production process has low potential to create core competencies. Failure to identify and resolve these shortcomings points, in the first instance, to deficiencies in expertise and experience within the organisation. Different expertise in the domain language and proficiencies in its application are required for different decision making applications. A practicing expert with knowhow provides proficiency in both the domain language and experience from its repeated successful application. On the other hand, commissioning agents need only to know the language to make simple decisions in following instructions. The level of expertise is gauged from: credentials (can talk); and experience (can meaningfully interact); and track record (can reliably do).

Production processes that deliver low average unit cost achieve this because declining cost economies are being realised. Sources of declining cost economies are:

- Economies of scale.
- Aligning the interests of the parties to a transaction.
- The law of large numbers.
- Economies from aggregation.
- Information asymmetries.

Chapter 3
The imitability of core competencies

Alternative activity types used by competitors

The value network map identifies the place and market position of competitors. Whether these competitors are using the same or different activity types provides information on the ability to replicate an organisation's core competencies. A high degree of industry knowledge is required to comment on the different activity types used by competitors. As a general observation, few activity types are present in mature industries, or where an industry is narrowly defined. An expansive definition of an industry will identify a wider range of activity types. Industries in transition are likely to have a wide range of activity types challenging one another. In the example of a courier delivery service from Figure 2, there are many competitors operating with similar production processes, although the capacities in use may be quite different. Ostensibly, this indicates that it is easy to imitate the core competencies because alternative types of production processes can be used.

Here the issue for an organisation with core competencies is, whether there is an alternative business angle or imitation of the current product and production process that could undermine the value of the current core competency? The converse of this also applies for a challenger or new entrant; how do they bypass the need to replicate the core competencies of existing competitors to gain access to a perceived opportunity? There are four ways that the need for, and hence value of, an existing core competency can be diminished by the availability of alternatives:

- Replicating the current systems, processes and technology and operating them more efficiently.
- Within the activity type with core competencies, finding and developing different production processes which may involve using different inputs.
- Using a different activity type. For example, changing from an activity type that involves owning assets to one that acquires the capability under an outsource contract (or vice versa).
- Disruption of the market by innovating a profitable, new product and production process giving much better value-for-money.

The cost to find and institute an alternative is a measure of the size of the barrier to entry to acquire the alternative. Where the present value of this cost is less than the value of the core competency, then it could be worthwhile investing to acquire the alternative. This cost of entry places a constraint on the value of a core competence. Having said this, an organisation may possess several scarce resources in addition to core competencies that increase the barrier competitors face in challenging the organisation.

Placing the business angle in the value network

What this points to is that what is to be imitated depends on the product and production process giving effect to the business angle. Recall, as shown in Figure 5, to be considered by buyers, products must have a price and perceived benefit that places it below and/or to the right of the constant value-for-money frontier. Ways that this can be achieved are by lowering price and/or improving the perceived benefit.

Changing the product specifications can change the ways in which the product is used/consumed, and therefore the buyer's production process (where the buyer is an organisation). This can be illustrated using the business-to-business parcel delivery example. Where the product is a commodity courier service purchased by an organisation, it is typically remote from the organisation's sales and customer engagement function. At this distance from the customer, the organisation could see courier delivery as a commodity product where, subject to a minimum service standard, a courier company is chosen on price. A quite different perceived benefit is offered where the courier company provides the organisation's customers, in the case of a retailer, with delivery choice and certainty. To provide this application product the courier company needs to have integrated capabilities in messaging, scheduling and routing. If, because of this engagement with the store's customers, cost savings are achieved from improved delivery efficiency, then the delivery service moves to two degrees removed from the interface with the customer. In this position, the courier service is no longer a commodity product, but is a business partner enabling the store to provide a better service to its customers, and turning the store's online presence into an effective retail channel.

A finding to be drawn from this illustration is that a clear understanding is required of the business angle when considering the question of how a core competence is to be imitated. An implication of this, when the other scarce resources available to an organisation are also taken into consideration, is that the allocation of value added and market share in a value network is moulded around the available scarce resources.

Reliability and resilience in meeting business plans

Core competencies are under threat of imitation by competitors and new entrants, from changes in market context, and inappropriate decisions by management. Unfortunately, these occurrences may go unnoticed amongst the turmoil of day-to-day operations where management must address the unexpected from things going wrong. To weather these challenges, organisations need to be resilient. Resilience is the ability to cope with unexpected events. The indicator that management can address these challenges is reliability in meeting business plans.

The capabilities and information flows in use in an organisation can be identified as the functional actions to give effect to a high-level 'ideal' resilient production process that is adept at reliably meeting business plans. The ideal is derived by creating an influence diagram for the activity type operating within the market environment. An influence diagram considers eight elements, and the recursive and feedback information flows between them. Three of these elements are capabilities to use:

- Knowhow, systems, and processes to maintain on-going income earning ability.
- Functional knowhow, systems, and processes to perform actions to deliver outputs.
- Risk mitigation knowhow, systems, and processes to ensure business plans are realised.

The relationships between these elements and information flows are depicted in Figure 14. In an influence diagram knowhow, systems and processes to perform actions and conditions (placed on nodes); and transactions and information flows (placed on arrows) are the elements. The signature of a resilient organisation is seen in the information flows of the production process. The absence of this information point to low resilience. Organisations with low resilience cannot be expected to have on-going continuity and this will impact their value. However, the converse need not hold true. Organisations can have resources assigned to mitigate risk and identify ways to sustain on-going profitability, but they are ineffective. A common reason for this is that these resources are primarily engaged in 'desk research', and are disconnected from action in the market.

Figure 14 *Influence diagram of a high-level ideal resilient production process (applied to the product market perspective)*

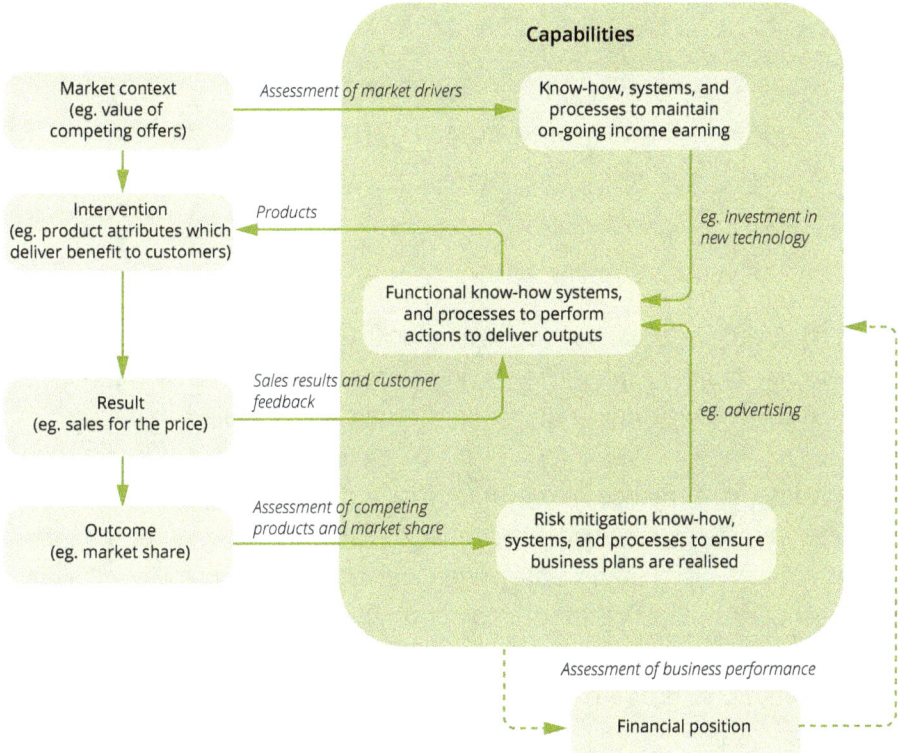

The actual information flows of a simple parcel delivery organisation are depicted in Figure 10. The match between the actual and ideal relationships from Figure 14 is assessed in Figure 15, and considers the extent to which there are:

1. Capabilities to:
   - maintain on-going income earning ability.
   - perform actions to deliver outputs.
   - ensure business plans are realised.

2. Transaction and information flows to:
- assess market drivers.
- deliver products.
- assess sales results and customer feedback.
- assess competing products and market share.
- assess business performance.
- put in place risk mitigation actions.
- put in place strategic options.

In this example, push/push coordination is used for the parcel delivery network, and the capabilities and information flows are almost exclusively centred on the coordination with customers and suppliers to deliver parcels. There are also information flows to support capabilities to assess business performance. However, absent are formal mechanisms to provide resilience to ensure that business plans are met, other than the insight of leadership to create options for on-going profitability. Also absent are supporting information to do this. The assessment shows the organisation to be focused on day-to-day operations, and achieving budgeted results as a parcel delivery service. There appears to be no focus on building core competencies.

Figure 15 *Assessment of the capabilities of a simple parcel delivery service*

Capabilities and supporting information flows	Leadership, strategy and communications	Finance and compliance	People capability and performance	Sales and customer relations	Operational capabilities	Conclusion
Capabilities						
Maintain on-going income earning ability						Absent
Perform actions to deliver outputs		Focus on managing accounts receivable and payable	Ensuring a supply of owner drivers	Focus	Focus	Resourced
Ensure business plans are realised	Focus					Resourced
Transaction and information flows						
Assessment of market drivers						Absent
Deliver products					Electronic manifests and parcel movement scanning	Resourced
Sales results and customer feedback				Focus		Resourced
Assessment of competing products and market share	Business-as-usual interaction with the market					Resourced
Assessment of business performance						Absent
Risk mitigation actions		Mainly compliance and insurance				Limited resource
Strategic actions		Capital budgeting decisions				Limited resource

Chapter 3

Making core competencies dynamic

The existence of the capabilities and its supporting information to provide an organisation with the resilience to reliably deliver its plans, whether these are formal or informal, provides little information on the breadth of the challenges that can be coped with, or speed of response. As discussed in the previous chapter, systems and processes have limits to their characteristics. This also applies to knowhow.

There is debate about the extent to which organisations should invest in the organisational ability to cope with uncertainty, nonetheless, it is now well recognised that the occurrence of unanticipated events is an integral component of business. Experience shows that organisations with organisational ability that is difficult to imitate are better equipped to deal with unanticipated events. There is also a view that people with knowhow, well connected to the market, supported by appropriate systems and processes, are best equipped to speculate and formulate responses to rare events. What is clear is that organisations are under continuous pressure to change. To cope with this change, organisations need cultures to facilitate continuous learning, and this requires investment in organisation wide continuous learning systems and processes.

Core competencies are difficult to imitate because they reliably deliver business plans and provide resilience

With adequate funding the components to replicate production processes, and market share can be bought. However, organisations that have the organisational ability to reliably meet business plans and have resilience to endure uncertain events are difficult to imitate. This is because they have systems and processes to: maintain on-going income earning ability; perform actions to deliver outputs; and ensure business plans are realised. This proficiency to deal with expected events is provided by instituted capabilities with supporting information. The signature of this potential is seen in the organisation possessing the 'ideal' resilient systems and processes. Here performance measurement has an important role to play to keep improving this potential.

The potential to cope with uncertainty is more difficult to assess, but two comments are worth making. First, the more distant people with responsibility for making decisions to respond to unplanned situations are from the frontline, the less effective they are in responding – this is the well acknowledged ineffectuality of strategic planning functions in organisations. Second, organisations that have a culture of continuous learning to advance knowhow are better placed to formulate responses to uncertainty.

Chapter 4
Rarity of core competencies

Creating choice to increase the value of core competencies

Core competencies are rare where they are in short supply to participants (or would be participants) because they are already being used in the most valuable production process available. Continuing to employ them in this way delivers the highest possible value. Competitive responses can compromise the rarity of core competencies. Consequently, rare core competencies also have a high degree of prolongation. In saying this, a resource that is rare and in short supply exposes the resource to competitive forces and takeover threats, such that the market value of the resource is at or above its FCF value. For this to be true, then for core competencies to be rare, they need to maintain their on-going income earning ability. This is achieved by the organisational ability to maintain a portfolio of salient options. In the context of core competencies this will be, a portfolio of real options.

A real option is the right but not the obligation to undertake some business action, such as constructing or selling a building. A real option can be created by buying land for the future construction of a building if conditions are right. The option to construct a building on the land is a real call option (the right to use the asset), and selling the land is a real put option (the right to extinguish the use of the asset through its sale). There are costs and benefits to holding the option open. Having bought land to create an option to build in the future, costs are incurred by continuing to own the land because of the time value of money and other costs incurred while it is vacant. This cost declines over time as the remaining time before sale/construction diminishes. Offsetting this is the benefit of holding land in the location which can proceed at the timing of the owner's choice should construction go ahead. The option ceases to exist when the decision is executed to sell or build. The expected cost and benefit of options including the option premiums are included in the calculation of business value.

Building and maintaining a portfolio of salient options for a sustainable business is about creating a choice of alternative valuable business angles. This brings focus to exploiting core competencies, and jettisoning capabilities and information that do not facilitate and support that. This is because capabilities and information that are peripheral to the main activity type add cost without contributing to enhancing value. In addition, management's attention can be diverted from the main tasks of the organisation by the demands of the peripheral, low value capabilities and information. This focus aims to avoid problems brought about through:

- Investing too little in maintaining and enhancing core competencies.
- Merger of businesses involving different activity types where the different activity types are maintained and not reengineered to enhance core competencies.
- Business transformation programmes that undermine the activity type and its declining cost economies. For example, by the implementation of outsourcing arrangements or inappropriate labour models.
- Business restructuring that aims to remove easy costs even where they undermine core competencies.

Against this background, the objectives in exploring ways to improve the value of core competencies should be made explicit. This might simply be to reaffirm a single-minded drive for an organisation to 'stick to its knitting' as the means to increase value. Alternatively, it could be the start of a journey to better understand other strategic directions the organisation could pursue.

Development strategies as real options

Development strategies are the different ways to parlay core competencies into new business angles and are the means to create salient options. Once developed, there are five high-level directions that businesses with existing core competencies can use them to create new business angles:

- Direction A - Growing market value for existing products.
- Direction B - Expanding into new products that enhance existing core competencies.
- Direction C - Vertical integrating with a buyer or supplier stage of the value network.
- Direction D - Transforming business processes with no change to products.
- Direction E - Repositioning a core competency by spin-off into a new business angle.
- Direction F - Rationalising by withdrawing from poor performing areas of the organisation.

Doing more of the same by growing market share (Direction A) may be accompanied by, because of the increased size of the business, the need to build and invest in additional capabilities and supporting information - making the business more complex even though there is no change to the activity type. More complexity in customers, markets for the supply of inputs, and activity types and their attendant knowhow, systems and processes, and organisational structure. Expansion into allied markets (Direction B) may not change the activity type but additional capabilities with supporting information may be needed to underpin the increased product variety. Accessing new or increased volume may necessitate the institution of new production processes and this may be accompanied by the adoption of a new activity type. Changing the activity type is the explicit intent: through vertical integration (Direction C) to add capabilities and supporting information with the aim of building new competencies;

or to improve return on applied resources (Direction D) (with no substantial change to products). Direction E aims to reposition to a different place in the value network to pursue new market opportunities, and with that, the need to develop a new business angle. Organisations can also increase value by: withdrawing from some business angles with poor returns on market value; and the sale of assets that are worth more to others than the organisation (Direction F). Aside from Directions A and F, leveraging existing core competencies into new opportunities requires developing additional new organisational abilities. This is sometimes done in collaboration with other organisations who can bring existing but different core competencies to exploit the perceived opportunity.

Before progressing to explore the opportunities to parlay existing core competencies it is worthwhile first to assess the improvements that can be made to the existing core competencies. Creating real options is not the same as finding ways to generate more revenue from existing assets (including contractual commitments). For instance, an organisation with high brand recognition with a chain of retail stores adding a range of brand unrelated and lowly regarded products to its in-store product range may add revenue but does not enhance core competencies or indeed its brand. On the other hand, taking an online store and redesigning its value proposition by adding an integrated fulfilment and delivery service (Direction B) can dramatically increase the value of the online presence.

Figure 16 shows the scope of the change in the constituents of the business angle by each development strategy for an organisation with core competencies. The strategies are categorised by degree of knowledge about the production process and market characteristics. At a high-level, least risk is involved in Direction A as it involves production processes and markets of which the organisation has a high level of understanding. Direction B is dominated by market uncertainty but with some risk about the production process. Directions C and D face high risk about the production process and no change in the market being serviced. Direction E is the riskiest, involving both market and production process risk. Nonetheless, the change brought about by parlaying core competencies are invariably significant and require a scoping business plan to assess their feasibility.

Figure 16 *Scope of the change in the constituents of the business angle by development strategy with examples of high-level development strategies available to a simple parcel delivery organisation*

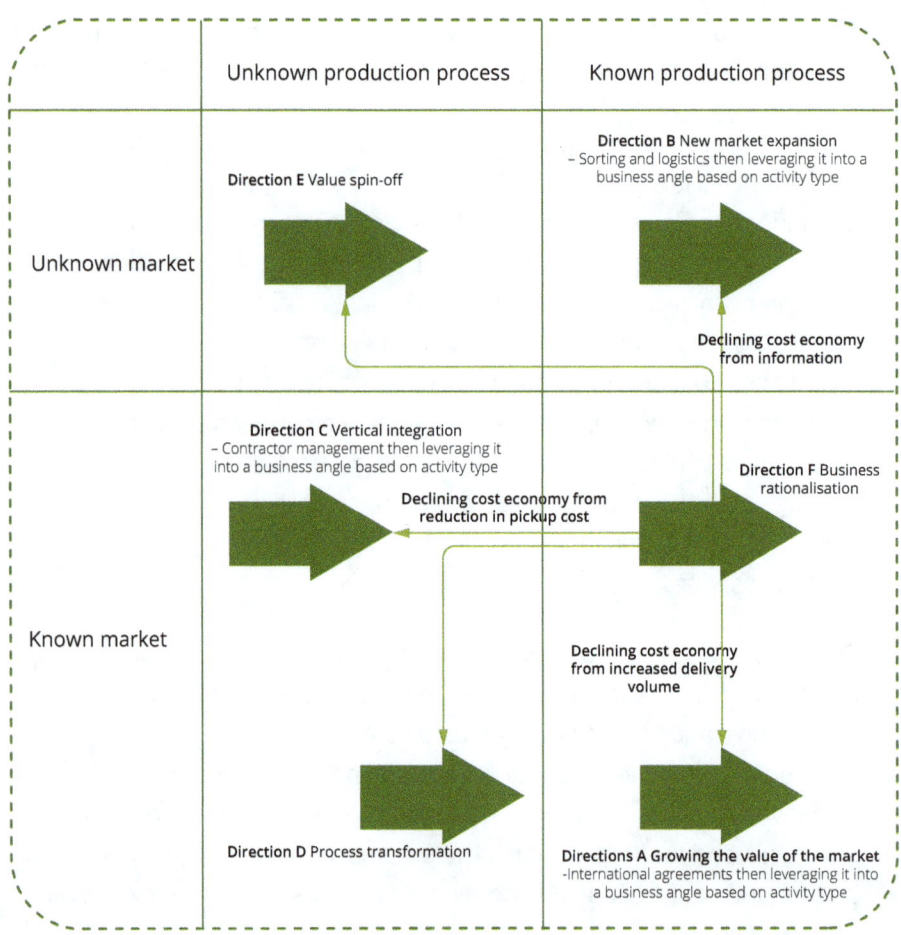

Direction A. Growing market share

The aim is to grow market share by exploiting economies that give declining cost advantage to the organisation. This includes growing market share by acquisition of other organisations with the same business angle. This strategy exploits the knowledge of both markets and production processes, and positive feedback effects that have been developed by the business. One way that market share can be acquired is through horizontal integration. Horizontal integration involves the acquisition of other organisations participating in the same business angle to gain additional capacity and access to new customers. In the context of core competencies, acquiring market share is of interest where it enhances core competencies by promoting declining cost economies (there are other concerns, but these are not considered here). A second way is to invest in production processes that provide the capacity and the benefits of declining costs to enable the organisation to be the lowest unit cost producer in the market, and then to price at a level to achieve sales at the planned output volume.

Considerations in growing market share are:

- How is increased market share to be gained – e.g. by acquisition or organic growth, and at what price?
- Which declining cost economies are to be promoted by increasing market share?
- Which capabilities with supporting information are to be expanded?
- What organisation wide systems and processes, and knowhow are to be exploited?
- What are the limits of the declining cost economies?
- How valuable are these economies?

Direction B. Expanding into new products that enhance existing core competencies

Knowledge of the product type and coordination mechanism is important because changing them is a source of new opportunities. The aim is to take capabilities with their supporting information that either have, or can become core competencies, and gain economies by expanding into allied markets, for example, by adding new products. On the one hand, this direction seeks to enhance existing capabilities and information, for example through declining cost economies, while on the other hand, facing the costs of creating new capabilities and supporting information.

In applying this development path, care needs to be taken in firmly grounding it in enhancing existing core competencies and not drawing superficial conclusions on the similarity between the processes involved. This direction should result in a reduction in the unit cost of the core product. In addition, the new business operating in the two markets should be profitable. The move of service stations into convenience stores is an example of an expansion into allied markets which could result in declining cost from better utilisation of the site. On the other hand, it is difficult to see any source of declining cost economies from the move, for example, of an air traffic control operator into airport luggage tracking.

Considerations are:
- What is the new market and product?
- What new capabilities and information will be invested in?
- What are the implications of these new capabilities to the activity type?
- Which declining cost economies are to be promoted by the expansion?

- What organisation wide systems and processes, and knowhow are to be exploited?
- What are the limits of the declining cost economies?
- How valuable are these economies to the core product?
- What is the value of the new expansion strategy?

Direction C. Vertical integrating with a buyer or supplier stage of the value network

The aim here is to drive a reduction in the cost of coordination by adding capabilities and information that result in a change in the activity type through vertical integration with supplier or buyer stages of the value network. Vertical integration is undertaken when there is a net reduction in transaction costs between the two stages in the value network by bringing them into the organisation. This requires the organisation developing or acquiring capabilities with supporting information in the preceding, or following, stages in the value network, and it results in a change to the type of activity type used by the organisation.

A commonly encountered use of this development strategy is for platform organisations to acquire the rights to applications products which extend the use of knowhow, systems and processes to new adjacent workflow processes or value networks by providing additional functionality. An example of this is a postal operator providing a letter scanning service that sends the scanned letter to the recipient by email. The cost saving from this is that the letter does not have to be delivered through the high cost physical delivery network.

Considerations are:

- What is the additional product, and who are the buyers?
- Which capabilities and information are to be added and what new activity type is being created?

- What are the implications of these new capabilities and information to the activity type?
- Which declining cost economies are to be promoted by the expansion?
- What organisation wide systems and processes, and knowhow are to be exploited?
- What are the limits of the declining cost economies?
- How valuable are these economies to the core product?
- What is the value of the new expansion strategy?

Direction D. Transforming business processes with no change to products

Changing the activity type to improve profit in current product markets. This is done by changing either or both the output delivery and input acquisition methods. Changing activity type occur where organisations move from inhouse manufacturing to outsource manufacturing. This involves, say, a change from activity type a Provider (assemble-assemble) to activity type e Systems Integrator (assemble-assign).

Competitive advantage can be gained by changing activity type, by better matching the organisation's funding, return and risk profile with those of the organisation's owners, and enabling access to core competencies and other resources owned by others. There are, however, risks of changing activity type, for example: reputational risk due to new relationships with buyers and suppliers, and the additional cost of uncertainty emanating from operating new production processes.

Business reengineering initiatives are frequently projects to change the activity type. For example, a manufacturer operating the assemble-assemble activity type moves to outsource its inputs, and in doing this is adopting an assemble-assign activity type. Were this manufacturer to go further and conclude that because of its strong brand, derived from its product design and marketing prowess, that all manufacturing and logistics is to be outsourced, then it would be adopting an arbitrage-assign activity type. Each of these changes in activity type changes the production processes used, and therefore the business model.

Considerations in redesigning the activity type are:

- What scarce resources, especially core competencies, does the organisation possess?
- Can value be significantly improved by changing the activity type?
- Is the change going to impact customers, products and their value proposition, price and sales?
- Which declining cost economies need to be stimulated and to what extent will these provide a competitive advantage?
- What are the required capabilities and information to achieve this?
- What knowhow, and organisational wide systems and processes are to be use?
- Can the core competency be made rare?
- How easily will this be able to be copied?

Direction E. Repositioning a core competency by spin-off into a new business angle

A value spin-off strategy involves moving into new markets that require investment in a new activity type, with the aim of repositioning at a higher value point in the value network. It is a high-risk strategy because it involves both a new market and new activity type. This is commonly achieved through strategic partnerships where two or more organisations enter into a cooperative agreement, such as a joint venture, to contribute specific scarce resources and funding to develop the market. Joint ventures involve the parties forming a new entity with each party having a stake and sharing in the returns. Special purpose vehicles are used where the relationship is for a specific project or for a limited duration (termination may be triggered by the occurrence of a specified event). This strategy is also pursued where an activity type proves to be ineffective and the business possesses other scarce resources, such as a well-known brand, trademarks, patents, or land, that can be leveraged into new business angles.

The intent of a strategic partnership is to improve the value of the existing organisation by:

- Enabling market entry by gaining access to other core competencies and other resources, for example distribution channels into new markets, in new locations; and intellectual property, brand, trademarks; and reputation (say, to circumvent hostile government regulations).
- Increasing unit gross margin, for example by better product design, stimulating declining cost economies, or removing costs, that would be hard to achieve when attempting to enter a new market alone.
- Risk sharing where there is much uncertainty and instability in entering a new market.

Considerations are:

- What objectives is the organisation trying to achieve through this strategy and how does a strategic partnership align with those objectives?
- What is the expected lifecycle of the opportunity and the strategic partnership, and what is the exit path?
- Which capabilities is the organisation trying to parlay through this strategy?
- Does each party contribute valuable scarce resources to the new entity?
- Does the new entity, with the contributions of all partners, have the requisite capabilities and information to be successful in the new market?

- How are declining cost economies to be promoted by entering the new market?
- How is risk being mitigated by forming the strategic partnership?
- How valuable is the proposed venture, and does it enable the organisation to achieve its objectives more effectively or more efficiently than other alternatives?
- What is the risk to the organisation by entering into this strategic partnership, for example, could it be taken advantage of by the other parties?

Direction F. Rationalising by withdrawing from poor performing areas of the organisation

The aim is to increase value by withdrawing from some business angles with poor returns on market value; and the sale of assets that are worth more to others than the organisation. Initiatives of this type are often undertaken as business turnaround initiatives to improve the short-term profitability of an organisation. Without a clear understanding that core competencies are scarce resources, these narrow-focused exercises run the risk of destroying core competencies in the drive to achieve short-term accounting profitability. If an organisation has no core competencies, then business turnaround initiatives are futile, and the business is worth no more than the liquidation value of its assets.

The central aim of restructuring line-of-business assets is: to identify and value the core competencies of the organisation; and separate these from assets worth more to others. This information is then used to develop actions to enhance the value of core competencies, while at the same time realising the value of poor performing assets. Considerations are:

- What scarce resources, especially core competencies, does the organisation possess?
- Is business resilience and the on-going income earning ability of the organisation compromised by disposing of the assets?

- Can value be significantly improved by disposing assets worth more to others?

Core competencies seed new salient options

Rarity is increased by parlaying core competencies into new business angles that increase the organisation's value. Core competencies are leveraged through development strategies. This is done by identifying core competencies, then exploring ways they can open new business angles with the potential to be real options. The benefits and costs from crafting development strategies is the option premium to keeping open the real option. With changing business conditions, management change the mix of options available to the organisation. Some options remain relevant and roll over from one period to the next, new options are acquired, while others will be exercised or allowed to expire. The composition of this portfolio of options is under continuous change, even where this is not explicitly managed. For a portfolio of salient real options founded on core competencies, the distinguishing feature is the unifying drive to realise declining cost economies.

An example of leveraging core competencies into new opportunities using the simple courier service discussed earlier is given in Figure 17. The activity type matrix maps how starting activity type g. Delivery services using contract drivers, with core competencies in:

- Contractor management then leveraging it into a business angle based on activity type c. Integrated delivery and fulfilment service - Direction C.
- Systems integration then leveraging it into a business angle based on activity type h. Marketer of branded small item logistic services – Direction B
- Sorting and logistics then leveraging it into a business angle based on activity type f. Network of nodes with as a transport backbone for other courier providers – Direction A.

Each of these development strategies is a real option created by possessing a core competency. They are real options because the core competency creates a right but not the obligation to undertake the development of a new business angle. The option to invest in the new business angle is a real call option, and diminishing the capability through underinvestment or cost cutting is a real put option. Costs are incurred to maintain and enhance the core competency. The benefit of maintaining and enhancing the core competency is from establishing the new business angle. The option ceases to exist when the decision is executed or abandoned.

Continuing this example, a portfolio of salient real options founded on core competencies could be centred on promoting declining cost economies from:

- Direction C - Integrated delivery and fulfilment service, however, there is no obvious source of declining cost economy being promoted.
- Direction A - Marketer of branded small item logistic services. Increase in delivery volume could promote declining cost economies in the delivery network.
- Direction A - Network of nodes as a transport backbone for other courier providers. Here declining cost economies are from reduced transaction cost due to pick-up of items from customers' premises which are returned to base for sorting and delivery.

The development strategies can be used to create real call options for: capital investment decisions; planning for new business angles; guiding response to changes in market conditions; and identifying takeover targets and strategic partners. Real put options can be created using Direction D to dispose of assets, and closing operations because of an absence of core competencies.

Figure 17 *Activity type matrix showing alternative business angles for a courier business*

Method of acquiring inputs	Method of delivering outputs			
	Rights pass with the product	Access to a network or capacity	Exploits law of large numbers	Easy access other products
Uses factors of production	a.	b.	c. Integrated delivery and fulfilment service	d.
Contracted for	e.	f. Network of nodes with as backbone for other courier providers	g. Delivery service using contract drivers	h. Marketer of branded small item logistic services
Risk being passed	i.	j.	k.	l.
Purchase for on-sale	m.	n.	o.	p.

The bones of an emerging corporate strategy founded on real options for the simple courier business is depicted in Figure 16. At a high level, two of the development strategies (those involving Direction B) involve unknow markets and unknown production processes, and one requiring the organisation to acquire new production process (Direction C). Having identified the strategic direction, initiatives are then developed to give effect to it. These in turn influence capital budgets, and the creation of additional real options – contributing to the curation of a portfolio of salient real options.

Rare core competencies keep on giving

Rarity from core competencies that provide real options managed as part of the portfolio of salient real options increases the rarity of core competencies. Real options are created by using existing core competencies to create new business angles by:

- Direction A - Growing market value for existing products.
- Direction B - Expanding into new products that enhance existing core competencies.
- Direction C - Vertical integrating with a buyer or supplier stage of the value network.
- Direction D - Transforming business processes with no change to products.
- Direction E - Repositioning a core competency by spin-off into a new business angle.
- Direction F - Rationalising by withdrawing from poor performing areas of the organisation.

What emerges from this is that managing core competencies as real call options creates the potential for a sustainable future for the organisation, whereas ignorance of core competencies effectively creates a portfolio of real put options and consigns the organisation to have a limited life expectancy.

Chapter 5

Managing a portfolio of salient real options as corporate strategy

When asked: "what is the source of profit?", most people answer that it is the difference between revenue and costs. While that is how to calculate profit, profit is derived from scarce resources and speculation.

Core competencies are a scarce resource formed in the production process used to supply products to exploit a perceived opportunity. Core competencies can be created in any of the contributors to profit. On the one hand, the information to answer this question therefore requires detailed, process engineering level understanding of production processes, coupled with insights about the market. It requires the linking of operational knowledge with knowledge of the management of business value.

On the other hand, earning profit necessitates the management of uncertainty. There is uncertainty in each of the markets a business operates, there is uncertainty in the operation of production processes, and uncertainty in the business environment. Core competencies have the organisational ability to provide resilience and reliability to deliver plans in the face of this uncertainty. Core competencies enable the organisation to generate more value than competitors. The value of core competencies is the value of the organisation.

Corporate strategy addresses how scarce resources are to be created, enhanced, and applied operationally; the competitive actions to be taken; and the timing and scope of strategic decisions. As decisions are executed, the portfolio of options and mitigants changes, and so do the option and uncertainty premiums. The maintenance of options and mitigants comes at a cost, the payback is from the increase in value from improved future returns and certainty of achieving plans and budgets. The inclusion of option and uncertainty premiums in budgets and strategic plans gives recognition to the portfolio of salient strategic options, risk mitigation arrangements and constraints that the business faces in participating in markets.

Corporate strategy involves continuously exercising numerous options and mitigants. Core competencies can be parlayed into new opportunities by creating real options. Real options created by core competencies underpin strategies to:

- Grow market value for existing products - Direction A.
- Expand into new products that enhance existing core competencies - Direction B.
- Vertical integrate with a buyer or supplier stage of the value network - Direction C.
- Transform business processes with no change to products - Direction D.
- Reposition a core competency by spin-off into a new business angle - Direction E.
- Rationalise by withdrawing from poor performing areas of the organisation - Direction F.

Core competencies used in this way are rare and difficult to imitate.

Organisations can fail to realise the potential of their production processes to form core competencies for reasons such as:

- Mismatch of activity type and perceived opportunity with the business angle, and inconsistency with the business objectives.
- Mismatch of the production process to the characteristics of the market (including its dynamic characteristics).
- Inconsistencies in the production process with the activity type, and

therefore not being able to realise the sources of declining cost economies.
- Inadequate information flows in the production process to enable the organisation to reliably deliver on plans and provide resilience in the face of uncertainty.
- Inappropriate level of expertise for the production process.
- Absence of organisational wide systems that deliver declining cost economies.
- Inability to parlay a position.

Core competencies can create real options to form the foundation of corporate strategy. Managing a portfolio of salient real options requires identifying core competencies and evaluating their current and potential value. However, core competencies can be improved or undermined by changes: in the value network; from management decisions; or imposed by social, economic and environmental conditions. These changes impose uncertainty on an organisation. In the face of uncertainty, real options, built on core competencies give the ability to profit from speculation due to this uncertainty. Core competencies are therefore both the source of value of an organisation, as well as providing the ability to profit from speculation.

Key influences on the work

Jay Barney is a key writer on core competencies and their value to a business and the VRIO framework. See for example the 2001 article 'Is the resource-based 'view' a useful perspective for strategic management research? Yes' published in *Academy of Management Review*.

The decision tree at the centre of the approach to identifying core competencies set out in Figure 1 is derived from Janice Black and Kimberly Boal in 'Strategic Resources: Traits, Configurations and Paths to Sustainable Competitive Advantage' a paper in the *Strategic Management Journal* of 1994.

Aswath Damodaran provides a full account of the FCF method of valuation in *Investment Valuation: Tools and techniques for determining the value of any asset*, first published in 1996.

The discussion on what constitutes knowhow is drawn from the work of Harry Collins, see for example Harry Collins and Robert Evans in *Rethinking Expertise* published in 2007.

The idea underlying the use of profile analysis to compare the alignment of the attributes of a production process to the type of process was stimulated by Terry Hill, and presented in his 1983 book *Production/Operations Management* published by Prentice-Hall International: London.

An explanation of the reasons for the mismatch between technology and its use is given by Brian Arthur in *The Nature of Technology: What it is and How it Evolves* (2009).

For more details of the ideas expressed in this guide see Robert Hughes, *The Drive of business: Strategies for Creating Business Angles*, published in 2016.

Consulting projects undertaken by Hughes Consulting Limited have informed the examples used in the text.

Glossary

Activity type – Activity type is the specific method used in the production process to transform acquired inputs into delivered outputs.

Agency costs – Agency costs are a specific type of transaction cost that arises when the interests of the agent are misaligned to those of the principal. These costs include the agent using the principal's resources for their own benefit, costs such as monitoring, and incentives and sanctions to align the interests of the agent with those of the principal, and the risk the principal faces from non-performance by the agent.

Agent – Agents and principals are the parties to a contractual arrangement in which the principal sets the terms and conditions to be fulfilled by agents. Suppliers are agents.

Aggregate method – Aggregate method provides products by operate capabilities using the knowhow, systems and processes that depend on the law of large numbers and scale-free infrastructure networks.

Application products – Application products extend the use of knowhow, systems and processes to new adjacent workflow processes or value networks by providing functionality.

Arbitrage method – Arbitrage method applies knowhow, systems, and processes to identify differences in the price of products and resources that are caused by asymmetries in information and high transaction cost. This method relies on transaction specific knowledge, which can arise from barriers to information, location, time, customer relationships, etc.

Assemble method – Assemble method uses knowhow, systems, and processes to produce products by exploiting economies of scale and scope.

Asset – 1. Assets are products with positive value that the organisation has rights of ownership or control.
2. Assets are stocks of benefits and include tangible assets (e.g. land, building, machinery, tools, and inventory) and intangible assets (e.g. goodwill, patents, working capital and bank accounts). Assets may not have a market value and are recorded in the Balance Sheet following GAAP.

Assign method – Assign method produces products using knowhow, systems, and processes to operate capabilities that gain efficiencies by improving coordination, by ensuring close alignment of the interests between principals and agents.

Benefit – Benefit is derived from product attributes that can be real, service attributes and include intangible benefits from product meaning, brand association, fashion, and bandwagon effects, to name a few.

Brand – Brand refers to notoriety and reputation. Positive brand can be associated with ease of access to buyers and providers, lower transaction costs, increased transactions, and higher margins. Brand is frequently equated to a person, product, organisation, or idea.

Business – Business is any entity engaged in exploiting a business angle. A business can be a business unit within an existing corporate, a new start-up venture, consortium, joint venture, or a businessperson operating on their own account. A business may or may not be constituted as a legal entity, such as a limited liability company or cooperative society, amongst other forms.

Business angle – A business angle is a perceived opportunity and an activity type to exploit it.

Business model – The business model is the way in which the business opportunity is converted into profit. This covers the activity type including its knowhow, systems and processes, organisational structure, product specifications, and target buyers.

Business opportunity – Business opportunity is an intervention in a market to potentially earn profit.

Capability – Capabilities utilise resources and supporting information through the application of knowhow, systems, and processes to perform actions that contribute to the functions of an organisation. Capabilities and supporting information contribute to the methods used to acquire inputs and deliver products.

Capability product – The provision of production processes able to perform functions to a specification.

Capacity – Capacity is the output volume that can be produced by a capability with its supporting information. Capacity is limited by knowhow, systems, and processes to perform functional actions and input resources.

Capacity products – The provision of production processes capable of producing an amount of product to a specification.

Capital – Capital is the funds provided by lenders and investors. The price of capital from lenders is the interest rate charged. The return to investors is a share of profits such as dividends.

Commodities – Commodities are consumed in production processes. Commodities include resources such as labour effort, electricity, and leases on property. Commodities are usually purchased using market and bilateral contracts.

Competitive advantage – Competitive advantage is the value that is attributed to scarce resources and is measured by FCF value. High competitive advantage is associated with high FCF value of scarce resources – which incorporate the ability to generate profits in the future – for the expected sales.

Complete products – Complete products are a catchall for all remaining products (that are not capability or capacity products) that includes commodities, other tangible assets, financial assets such as a promise to pay, and other intangible assets such as intellectual property rights.

Continuous learning – Continuous learning results from organisation wide systems and processes for systematically codifying new information to build a body of knowledge to enhance core competencies and the profit from speculation.

Contractual commitments – Contractual commitments is a catchall category for items that arise from express terms and conditions between the parties to an agreement, sometimes in the form of a legally binding agreement and which are not otherwise classified as commodities and assets. Contractual commitments are intertwined with the organisation's dealings in all element markets. Importantly contractual claims can create assets as well as liabilities for the organisations. These contracts can be bilateral or trilateral. GAAP and tax authorities have specific rules for the treatment of some contractual commitments.

Contributor expertise – The state of expertise to contribute to profit. This requires the ability to reliably formulate solutions by doing complex calculations in a wide variety of applications within the domain, explain the choice of calculation to arrive at that solution, and reliably execute those solutions.

Contributors of value – There are five contributors that can improve FCF value. They do this by: improving the value-for-money of products that leads to improved revenue (Contributor 1); improving the selection and purchase of inputs that result in lower input costs (Contributor 2); improving the productivity and effectiveness of the production process to enhance scarce resources (Contributor 3); improving the use of appropriate risk mitigants to ensure that business plans are met, and improving the use of strategic options to extend the on-going profitability of the organisation (Contributor 4); and improving financial management so that it adds to the value of the organisation (Contributor 5).

Coordination mechanism – Products are exchanged according to the coordination mechanisms used between the parties. There are four types of coordination mechanism. Push/push coordination involves the supplier producing products as a precursor to offering them for sale in the market. Push/pull coordination is the production for inventory, that is subsequently drawn down by buyers, or where capacity or capability are put in place to be called on when required. Pull/pull relates to customised production when a product is produced to meet a custom order. Pull/push production is contract production for a buyer's inventory, from which the buyer then draws down their requirements.

Core competency – A core competency is a capability or set of capabilities with supporting information that contribute to the creation of positive FCF value for the organisation.

Declining cost economies – Declining cost economies are positive feedback effects that create value added through lower average costs, increasing barriers to entry or lower transaction costs, and include those derived from size, scale and scope achieved in the operation of knowhow, systems, and processes; agency costs, the law of large numbers, scale-free infrastructure networks and density economies; asymmetries in access to information, knowledge, institutional arrangements, and location and time.

Demand curve – A demand curve shows the relationship between price and the quantity of a product bought.

Development strategies – Strategies used to launch initiatives to open new business angles within a value network: growing market share (Direction A), expansion into allied markets (Direction B), changing the activity type through vertical integration (Direction C), changing the activity type to improve profit in current product markets (Direction A), and expanding into new markets that require investment in new activity types.

Domain – A domain is an area of responsibility able to create and maintain core competencies and manage the premium for uncertainty. Domains are frequently defined by areas of research, and social and institutional definitions, for example, engineering and marketing.

Domain knowledge – Expertise related to a domain.

Enterprise – Synonym for business.

Exchange products – Exchange products provide a high degree of readiness for use, through for example, custom, standardisation and specification, and transfer decision-making rights to consume or use to the buyer on sale, if not entirely, then at least for a period.

Expected profit – Expected profit is the planned for profit based on estimates of income, less costs including the premiums for uncertainty and options.

Expertise – Expertise refers to the ability to create and build core competencies. Contributor expertise is the knowhow suitable for being/contributing/creating a core competence. Interactional expertise is a low state of expertise suitable for working with other domains to build core competencies. Primary source knowledge is a lower level of expertise suitable for making simple decisions in following instructions. General knowledge is a still lower level of expertise.

FCF – Free cash flow – see profit.

FCF value – FCF value is calculated as the net present value of expected future free cash flows.

Feedback effects – Feedback effects refer to the nature of the interrelationship between the attainment of one state (e.g. volume produced) and value of another state (e.g. cost structure). Feedback effects can be supply and demand-side effects and the impact can be positive, negative, or neutral. For example, with the production of more output the impact of positive feedback is declining average costs and negative feedback would result in increasing average costs.

GAAP – Generally Accepted Accounting Principles.

Gross margin – Gross margin is profit to sales revenue (ProfitSales) expressed as a percentage.

Heuristic market supply curve – A heuristic market supply curve shows the estimated costs and market shares achieved by the participants in the market compared to the price for a product.

Inference diagram – An inference diagram shows the relationship between initiatives to address critical assumptions underpinning the business opportunity, the performance of the essential core competencies, critical success factors, and key drivers and their impact on cash flow.

Information – Information covers data, details, facts, and knowledge about a situation.

Information asymmetries – Information asymmetries refer to situations where one party has better information than others and this causes the parties to behave differently. Information asymmetries arise from constraints on access to data, deficiencies in knowledge, from institutional arrangements, from geographic location, and because of time.

Innovation – Innovations are improvements instigated by an organisation in any of the five contributors to FCF value.

Inputs – In the setting of the definition of profit, an input is any cash expenditure such as on commodities and assets.

Interactional expertise – To work with other capabilities there should be interactional expertise as well – this is a lower level of expertise that enables domains to work together, and requires a level of understanding of that other domain. To be effective, interactional expertise, nonetheless, requires a level of expertise in that other domain, such as, to routinely do simple calculations (apply 'rules of thumb') from that other domain.

Interface products – Interface products are associated with the interaction with systems and processes, or channel for delivering exchange products.

Investment – The commitment of assets, including capital, resources, labour (such as in sweat equity) and reputation to an organisation.

Knowhow – Knowhow is the domain specific expertise and experience that can be applied to specified capabilities to profit from scarce resources and speculation.

Knowledge illusion – Overestimate of level expertise frequently brought about by self-referencing performance assessment from a narrowed codification of expertise, a history of poor investment in analytical and evaluation capability, and lack of testing in the market or from external peer review.

Law of large numbers – The phenomenon where, with more occurrences of an unconnected event, the occurrence of an event lies more closely to the average occurrence of the event.

Market – A market is the institutions, social conventions, infrastructure, and capabilities that facilitate the repeated exchange of products, assets, skills, capital, information, and other resources.

Market context – Market context is an umbrella term for the situation that applies to a particular market, including its size, suppliers and buyers, the products, and societal expectations, institutional arrangements, and cultural norms in which it operates.

Market disruption – A market disruption is a buyer experience that occurs when comparative value-for-money changes rapidly enough to be noteworthy, forcing a re-evaluation of spending patterns.

Market value – Market value is the price obtained for a product or asset in a fair sale. When applied to the business it is the value of the business as a going concern.

Method – Method is a set of capabilities with supporting information enabling the acquisition of inputs or delivery of outputs.

Option – An option confers the right, but not an obligation, to undertake a certain course of events. A tradeable option contract involves the purchaser of the option paying a fee for the right to buy (called a call option) or sell (this is a put option) a real or financial asset at a specified price. A real option is the right but not the obligation to undertake some real business activity. Unlike tradable option contracts, real options, in general, cannot be traded as securities and may not be precisely time bound. The term option is used in two ways:

1. Strategic options which provide the capacity to respond to uncertain events so as to provide on-going continuity for the organisation.

2. Tactical options that address short term variations due to events such as price fluctuations.

Option premium – The option premium is the resource allocated to maintain and enhance the on-going income earning ability of the organisation.

Organisation – Organisation refers to any entity engaged in economic activity to exploit a business angle. In this setting, an organisation can be a business unit within an existing corporate, a new start-up venture, consortium, joint venture, or a businessperson operating on their own account. An organisation may or may not be constituted as a legal entity, such as a limited liability company or cooperative society, charity, amongst other forms.

Organisational ability – Organisational ability refers to knowhow and the operation of organisation wide systems and processes.

Organisational structure – The organisational structure refers to knowledge acquisition, business strategy, organisational architecture, and incentive schemes.

Outputs – In the setting of the definition of profit, an output is any cash income, most importantly products. Some outputs are inputs that are resold.

Participants – Participants are involved with an organisation and in a value network, including buyers, providers, suppliers, competitors, and government.

Parties – Parties are the participants in a transaction that involve contractual claims, such as buyers and their suppliers, and principals and agents. For example, there are parties to a contract and participants in a market.

Perceived benefit – The benefits to the buyer including aspirational benefits in the form of its product meaning, such as its allure within the culture and context in which the product is offered for sale.

Platform – A platform is a highly scalable production process that removes a set of shared transaction costs faced by large groups of users.

Premium for uncertainty – The premium for uncertainty is the cost to cope with the unexpected in order to realise business plans and budgets. The cost consists of risk mitigants and the consequences to flow from the occurrence of uncertain events.

Principal – See explanation for agents. A buyer is a principal.

Product – Product is used as a generic term for items that are exchanged between parties in product markets and have attributes that provide benefits such as service quality.

Product meaning – Product meaning refers to how buyers relate to a product because of connotations associated with its physical, functional, symbolic, and cultural attributes.

Product specification – The product specification describes the product form, type of interconnection with the production processes, and coordination mechanism, as set out in the technical, functional and performance attributes, the amounts, and the terms and conditions of the contract.

Product type – Product type is a description of of interconnection with the production process. Exchange, interface, and application products are different product types.

Production process – The production process is the overarching term for the collection of capabilities and supporting information used by the organisation. A production process has organisational structure, activity type that uses production technology with appropriate knowhow, systems and processes, resources, and contractual obligations to transform a volume of inputs into outputs.

Profit – Profit during a period is the net operating profit after tax, less the change in working capital and expenditure required to maintain the operating profit. This definition of profit is also known as free cash flow. An approximation of free cash flow from the financial accounts of a business is EBIT (1 – tax rate) plus depreciation and amortization less change in working capital less expenditure to maintain the current operating capability.

Profit margin – Profit margin is the ratio of profit to sales revenue.

Real options – See options.

Resource – A resource is a source or supply of profit. To illustrate this concept, whereas real estate property is an asset, the flow of benefits it provides (e.g. shelter, prestige) is a resource. The asset can be sold. By letting real estate the resource is sold. Other examples of resources are labour effort and knowhow.

Return from speculation – The return on speculation is the contribution to profit to recognise the gain or loss from changes in product and asset prices, and other inputs from participating in the market.

Risk – 1. The variation from the target value that is anticipated, and its consequences assessed. Risk is management's expectation of the variation, but is only one component of uncertainty. Before the event it is impossible to know the degree to which risk is aligned to the uncertainty.

2. Synonym for uncertainty, connoting exposure to loss which, for example, could result in loss of capital invested.

Scale-free infrastructure networks – Scale-free infrastructure networks relates to production processes, especially infrastructure networks, which involve high initial fixed cost and diminishing unit costs, and which follow a power law relationship for the addition of more users.

Scarce resources – Scarce resources are distinguished from other assets by their price being established by their profit earning ability. Scarce resources include core competencies and can include physical assets, financial assets, and legal rights.

Speculation – Speculation is the act of picking a future price for a product or asset.

Strategy – A set of directed actions to realise an objective.

System – 1. A network of capabilities and information flows with resultant behaviour responses to external stimuli. In this meaning an organisation is a system, as is a value network.

2. The equipment, software, plant, machinery, infrastructure, and procedures used in processes following prescribed procedures, which provide the capability and capacity to deliver an organisation's outputs, for example a computer system.

Transaction costs – The costs incurred in the process of organisations transacting are transaction cost. These include searching, negotiating, changes to be able to use the product, ambiguity in scope of the product being contracted for, monitoring performance, invoicing and payment, maintaining documentation and performance failure.

Uncertainty – Uncertainty is the variation from the target value. Uncertainty ranges from risk (that is, the known unknowns in which the likelihood of events occurring can be assessed); through to acknowledgement of unknown knowns, for example, severe rare events where the potential for occurrence is recognised even though their occurrence may be unknown; and on through to unknowable events. These events can occur in all contributors to business value and cover uncertainty in price, opportunity, input, capability, decision, business value, and regulatory and institutional arrangements.

Value – That is business value of FCF value - see FCF value.

Value added – Value added is the difference between the benefit enjoyed by buyers from a product less the cost to produce it. Value added is the sum of the value-for-money to buyers plus the profit to suppliers.

Value controller – An organisation with high bargaining power that exerts a high degree of control over the allocation of value added in a value network can dictate, at least for a period, the pace of change in the value network.

Value network – Value network is a network of capabilities and supporting information, usually from more than one organisation, which culminates in the capacity to deliver products to the final consumer.

Value network map – A value network map is a depiction of the stages in a value network, the participants at each stage as measured by their market share, and the relationship between the participants.

Value proposition – Value proposition is the promise that a product will deliver perceived benefits to the buyer for the price.

Value-for-money – Value-for-money is the difference between the perceived benefit to the buyer of a product and its price.

Value-for-money indifference curve – The value-for-money indifference curve describes the relationship between price and the perceived benefit of the product.

Venture – A business with the connotation of a high speculative component for expected profit.

VIRO model – The VIRO model holds that a capability and its supporting information have the strongest case for being a core competency where it is valuable, costly to imitate, rare and derived from organisational ability to exploit them. Where any of these conditions do not hold then the capability has low potential for being a core competency.